You
DIDN'T MISS IT!

God's Best Is Worth the Wait

WENDY GRIFFITH

You Didn't Miss It! God's Best Is Worth the Wait
Trilogy Christian Publishers A Wholly Owned Subsidiary of Trinity Broadcasting Network

2442 Michelle Drive Tustin, CA 92780

Rights Department, 2442 Michelle Drive, Tustin, CA 92780.

Trilogy Christian Publishing/TBN and colophon are trademarks of Trinity Broadcasting Network.

Cover design by: Grant Swank

For information about special discounts for bulk purchases, please contact Trilogy Christian Publishing.

Trilogy Disclaimer: The views and content expressed in this book are those of the author and may not necessarily reflect the views and doctrine of Trilogy Christian Publishing or the Trinity Broadcasting Network.

Manufactured in the United States of America

10 9 8 7 6 5 4 3 2 1

Library of Congress Cataloging-in-Publication Data is available.

ISBN: 979-8-88738-731-4

E-ISBN: 979-8-88738-732-1

*To my Heavenly Father, who was faithful to fulfill His promises,
to my husband, Bill, who was definitely worth the wait,
and to those who are still waiting:*

You Didn't Miss It!

Acknowledgments

First, I'd like to thank the readers of my first book, *You Are a Prize to Be Won! Don't Settle for Less Than God's Best*. I cherished every email, Facebook, Twitter, and Instagram message you sent me. Thank you for sharing your hearts with me and for your amazing and encouraging feedback! You showed me that God can take our worst heartache and use it for good and somehow bless others in their own journeys. You also asked me to write the "next chapter"—the rest of the story and the happy ending. This book is for you.

I'd also like to give special thanks to Vanessa Lancellotti. I was assigned to be her mentor through a Regent University program, but she became mine and encouraged me to keep writing. Vanessa, God sent you into my life at just the right time, and I am eternally grateful.

I'd also like to thank Jemimah Wright, Stacy Hord Hulm, and Cheri Martin for sharing their incredible love stories in this book. You are further proof that good things can happen "late in the game" and that waiting on God is always worth it!

And Rhonda Gray, your love, friendship, prayers, and encouragement helped me to hold on and wait for God's perfect timing. That's why there's a whole chapter devoted to you, my friend!

Many thanks to my brother, Truman, for taking time to read and edit some chapters. You're the best, and I love you.

And to my husband, Bill. Without you, honey, there would be no happy ending and no love story to tell! You made the long wait so worth it. I will love you forever.

And to my Heavenly Father, who gave me the desires of my heart and will do the same for you. You didn't miss it!

Love,
Wendy

Praise for *You Didn't Miss It!*

"You Didn't Miss It!" is wonderfully entertaining! Wendy Griffith is truly the Bridgette Jones of Christian romance! Her personal experiences are insightful, masterfully written, and delivered with heartfelt emotion.

An uplifting spiritual read filled with faith and hope. Wendy never gave up on finding her soul mate, and after reading "You Didn't Miss It!" neither will you! I'm looking forward to bringing her delightful story to the silver screen!

—Tony Marinozzi
Screenwriter, Producer

Wendy Griffith's new book is one of the most encouraging, optimistic messages of our time! Like Wendy, my wonderful wife and I were in our fifties before we were divinely aligned as perfect mates. We both thought love had passed us by! But, same as Wendy and her husband Bill, the best was yet to come. Their phenomenal series of Godwinks, weaving every step of their exciting relationship to a very compelling book, will lift the hearts of every reader and affirm that you, too, can claim hope for yourself!

—SQuire Rushnell and Louise DuArt Rushnell
Authors of The Godwink Book Series

If anyone can liken waiting for a husband to a great adventure, Wendy can! Full of twists and turns, sincerity, and humor, Wendy's journey is a testament to a woman's perseverance to wait on God and His faithfulness to those who trust Him. I've known Wendy throughout her journey, and once she received the revelation from God that she was a prize to be won, she committed to settling for nothing less than God's best for her. In a day when women have drifted from the truth of how valuable they are and, unfortunately in the process, robbed men of the joy and manhood of finding a prize worth fighting for, Wendy brings the vision back to life that God has wanted for His daughters all along: that women are a treasure and the men who recognize that will stop at nothing to get it.

—Stacy Hord Hulm
Speaker and Author of *A New Vision for Dating*

Wendy and her husband, Bill, have given us a gift in writing this book. Sharing their love story in such an open, generous way and helping us learn from the lessons they learned. Wendy and Bill's story reminds us that it is never too late, that God's timing is perfect, and that He speaks to His children. I loved Wendy's first book, "You Are a Prize to be Won!" and this sequel is a beautiful picture of her faith being rewarded in a way that was better than she could have asked or imagined! It's a love story you won't be able to put down!

—Jemimah Wright
Author of *Isabella's Voyage, Dare She Heed Hope's Call*

Wendy's inspirational love story is a powerful reminder that God is faithful to fulfill His promises. He heals our broken heart, redeems our past, and restores the years the locust has eaten. Wendy is a bold and refreshing example to women all around the world of what it means to remain faithful in the waiting and ultimately reap a bountiful harvest!

—Vanessa Joy Lancellotti
Certified Master Christian Life Coach
and Alumni Relations Officer at Regent University

"You Didn't Miss It!" will inspire every reader, male or female, to be faithful to God and to oneself and to trust God with all matters of the heart. Wendy's book does more than encourage the broken-hearted or those who have been disappointed in love. It offers both sides of the story—her own and her husband Bill's version of how God led them to the love of their lives. This is a remarkable story of love, healing, and adventure, a must-read for anyone who has grown weary in the search for love yet is unwilling to settle for anything less than God's best.

—Rev. Sherry Blackman
Author of *Tales from the Trail: Stories from the Oldest Hostel on the Appalachian Trail* and *REV-IT-UP, Tales of a Truck Stop Chaplain*

"You Didn't Miss It!" is an amazing, hope-filled, true story that will ignite your spirit to believe God and help you through the hope-deferred times of life, knowing that the desire shall come and be a tree of life (Proverbs 13:12)! Wendy is a God-appointed influencer sent to

strengthen and encourage people who are losing their "faith grip" on the hopes, dreams, and promises God has given them. Her message is, "Put your trust in the Lord! Our Father in heaven has strength for the weary and hope for the hopeless! God hears our prayers and will fulfill all of His faithful promises to us as we seek Him first and take Him at His Word!" Surely, He will do us good (Psalm 84:11)!

—Pastor Rhonda Gray
Grace Fellowship Church
Slidell, Louisiana

Contents

God Listened

"But God has surely listened and has heard my prayer."

Psalm 66:19 (NIV)

It was the last day of our honeymoon, the last few hours of our magical African safari in Tanzania. My new husband, Bill, and I were still caught up in the whirlwind of our beautiful wedding in the majestic hills of Southwest Virginia, surrounded by family and close friends, and now what had been a perfect honeymoon (minus the canceled flight to New York because of snow that rerouted us through Kenya). Still, it had been everything we dreamed of and more.

As we climbed into the van to be escorted back to Kilimanjaro International Airport after some last-minute souvenir shopping, our driver said, "Oh, look! You guys are lucky! You can see the mountain today!" And there it was! My beautiful, snow-capped Kilimanjaro poking out from a wreath of white fluffy clouds. The memories of climbing to the top of Africa's highest mountain years before I had met my new husband came flooding back. The tremendous effort it took to reach the summit, the feeling of victory at not turning back when I was so scared on summit night, and how climbing that mountain had helped me heal from a very painful past relationship.

"Would you like a photo?" our driver asked. "Sure!" we said. He pulled the van over, and we jumped out.

It was in that moment that I realized that this was truly a full-circle moment in my life. I remembered what the Holy Spirit whispered to my heart when I finished the climb back in 2014, "You win." Now, I knew what God meant as Bill and I stood holding hands and smiling with that beautiful summit towering over our heads. It was as if God was saying, "*Your struggle to reach the summit was not in vain, nor was your wait for this day.*"

As we continued to the airport, I asked our friendly Tanzanian driver, "What's your name?" He answered, "God Listened." I said, "No, what is your name?" thinking he misunderstood me. He said, "My name is God Listened. You see, my mother had to wait for me for a long time, and when I finally arrived, she named me God Listened." And after years of waiting for this moment, I knew that God, indeed, had listened to me too.

Dear reader, I didn't miss it, and neither have you! No matter how long you've waited for your heart's desire, no matter how old you are, no matter how much you think you've messed up and it's never going to happen for you, I'm here to tell you God is not finished writing your story. Your happy ending is still out there! I pray you will be encouraged by what God did for me because He's no respecter of persons, and what He did for me He can and will do for you. He loves you and wants to give you His very best.

I'm confident that by the end of this book you will know for certain what I now know—you didn't miss it!

1

You Didn't Miss It!

"And Let us not grow weary while doing good,
for in due season we shall reap if we do not lose heart."

Galatians 6:9

Years ago, when I was going through a painful break-up, I was out walking in my neighborhood, as I often do, when suddenly, I felt the Lord break into my thoughts with a clear word that hit my spirit like a bolt of lightning. He said, "*You didn't miss it*, Wendy, and it's not too late." I was forty-seven years old, never married, and feeling like my chances of finding marital bliss were growing dimmer by the day when the Lord stepped in with a new headline—*you didn't miss it!*

Tears of joy ran down my cheek. The Lord knew I was struggling to stay in faith, and with this one powerful phrase, He gave me new hope and new courage to keep believing, keep hoping, and keep trusting Him for His perfect timing.

If you're reading this, I believe this word is for you too—why? Because God is no respecter of persons—what He did for me, He can and wants to do for you. I don't care if you're thirty-five or seventy-five, God is faithful, and He's the author of second chances. So, right now, I'm telling you what God told me, "You didn't miss it, and it's not too late! Your best days are still ahead, and the thing you're believing God for—it will happen if you don't give up." (Galatians 6:9).

In Due Seson

When I first came to CBN as a young thirty-something woman, I was a reporter for Christian World News, and I would often ask my then-boss, Stan Jeter, an older, wiser, and happily married man, when I would meet my husband. I was good friends with him and his wife, Rhoda, and admired their godly relationship. He would always reply in his soothing and deep baritone voice, "In due season, Wendy, in due season." His calm assurance would give me hope to hold on for one more day. The good news is due season does come! Psalm 102:13 says, "You will arise and have compassion on Zion, (put your name here) for it is time to show favor to her – the appointed time has come. I love that – God has an appointed time to bless you and me and give us the desires of our hearts. Trust Him because what God has for you really is worth the wait and your due season could be closer than you think. But waiting is still hard! I get that. In this book, I'll share with you some lessons I learned and some things that I did that helped me to not grow weary in the waiting.

Everyone loves a happy ending; that's why you'll never see a Hallmark movie without one, for which I, for one, am very thankful.

I really don't like it when I invest a couple of hours watching a movie and it has a sad or unfulfilling ending. When I wrote my last book, *You Are a Prize to Be Won, Don't Settle for Less than God's Best*, out of hundreds of positive reviews, someone wrote, "I don't like the ending." In other words, she wanted the girl meets boy, the proposal, the wedding—and guess what, so did I! But God wasn't done writing my story. I wrote it when I was still single, going through heartbreak, and waiting on God to bring me His best. This book—*You Didn't Miss It!* —is the rest of the story! With the all-important happy ending. But what makes a happy ending even happier? When you've tasted the depths of heartbreak and despair and waited long past the point that you thought was humanly possible for God to answer your prayers, and then, finally, it happens! Then, your happy ending is even sweeter because you had to wait for it. This book is my happy ending — and for all of you who asked, "how did you meet your husband?" But first, there was the heartbreak.

I had never known this kind of heartache. Just breathing seemed hard. What was worse was the constant mental torment—what could I have done differently? Was it my fault that he broke up with me? Was God punishing me? Would I ever find love again? Even though we had only dated for a year, I was devastated when my ex-boyfriend broke up with me instead of proposing to me like I dreamed he would. If I'm honest, though, I think I knew deep down he wasn't "the one," but I wanted the fairy tale more than I wanted the truth. Specifically, I wanted the proposal, the bridal shower, the wedding, and the honeymoon, and I was tired of waiting. What I really feared more than anything was going back to my lonely weekends. Although work kept me busy Monday through Friday, I dreaded Friday afternoon when all my television shows were done, and my colleagues would shout, "Have a good weekend!" as they walked out the door to their husbands, wives, families, or significant others. The thought of going back to those lonely weekends was almost more than I could bear, but then I didn't really have a choice. The Lord had told me to "mourn and move on." I thought that was easy for Him to say, but I reminded myself that He is a good God, that He loves me and wants the best for me. Clearly, the relationship I had spent the last twelve months in was not His best.

Just a few weeks after the breakup, I heard the Holy Spirit say, "Write about your test." I thought it was interesting that God called my heartbreak a "test," and I was determined to pass the test, whatever it took. Go figure—the words just poured out of me onto the keypad, and the book *You Are a Prize to Be Won* was born. It's amazing to me how God can take your deepest, most personal pain, and when shared with others, can be the very thing they need to find hope and get back on their feet. I am so grateful for every person who wrote to me on social media or by email to let me know that my story helped them. One lady, who was in a very toxic relationship, told me my book even helped save her life! If you're going through heartbreak, please know God will never waste your pain. He won't waste one single tear—but you must give your pain to God. For me it was a daily going to the feet of Jesus and pouring out my heartache, my fears, and my questions to the Lord and then listening to His voice.

And that, my friends, is where the healing takes place—at the feet of Jesus and with every precious word that He whispers to your spirit.

God Wants to Give You His Best

The truth is, like any good father, God wants to give you His best! In 2014, about two years after the breakup, I was sitting on an airplane that was about to take off for Istanbul, Turkey. I was happy to be going on a mission trip with my good friend Marguerite where we would be praying for women from that part of the globe, some of whom were in very desperate situations. I was looking forward to ministering the love of Jesus to these precious women and taking a break from thinking about my own issues. Nevertheless, as I sat there waiting for take-off, my thoughts turned to what I still didn't have. I remember very clearly saying to the Lord, "*You know, Lord, I'm not getting any younger. Two years ago, things were a bit 'firmer,' and I feel like I gave him (the ex-boyfriend) one of my best years.*" Without hesitation, the Lord answered me back, "*That's right, Wendy, and now I'm going to give you My best.*" Drop the mic. Okay, God, You win.

We all want God's best, but few of us want to wait for it. If God had not stepped in and ended my previous relationship, I might have missed His best. But in His goodness and love for me, He did step in and, in the process of my heartbreak, taught me some profound lessons—mainly that I loved my ex-boyfriend but not myself. When you love yourself, you don't settle for bad behavior.

God is a God of order—and before I could be in a truly healthy relationship, I had to learn how to love myself. If that's where you are today, be encouraged, you didn't miss it either—maybe God just needs a little more time to teach you your incredible value, and trust me, it's a lesson worth learning and one that will prepare you for God's best. Now, if you want the back story, I recommend reading *You Are a Prize to Be Won* first. But if you want to go straight for the happy ending, then grab a cup of coffee or some popcorn—I'm about to tell you how God answered my biggest prayer and gave me my heart's desire and will do the same for you.

You didn't miss it!

2

The Inca Trail to Machu Picchu

How beautiful upon the mountains
Are the feet of him who brings good news,
Who proclaims peace,
Who brings glad tidings of good things,
Who proclaims salvation,
Who says to Zion,
"Your God reigns!"

Isaiah 52:7

Our love story began along the grassy slopes of the Inca Trail to Machu Picchu.

Well, sort of.

I was hiking in the Peruvian Andes with my good friend Ginna. Ginna is the kind of girl you might be tempted to be jealous of if she wasn't so nice and fun to be around. She's super accomplished, educated at Yale, lawyer by profession, gorgeous by nature, and a serious mountain climber, with three Kilimanjaro summits to her credit and several more summits higher than that. For several years, she also ran her own non-profit called "Climb for Conservation" and, in June of 2017, was co-leading this particular climb—a four-day trek through the Andes, including three nights sleeping in a tent, to the tall green peaks of Machu Picchu. Part of the money raised would go to help the endangered Peruvian black bear.

The weather in the Andes that June was nearly perfect—sunny and cool. The terrain was challenging, although nothing compared to my last two climbs: Mount Kilimanjaro at 19,341 feet and Kala Patthar in the Himalayas, which sits just above Everest Base Camp at 18,514 feet. The highest we would climb during this trek would be nearly 14,000 feet to an ominously named place called "Dead Woman's Pass." I didn't care much for the name but figured I'd survived much higher treks.

Ginna and I met on Facebook—thanks to a series of small miracles. While attending a Christmas party in December of 2016 with my lawyer friend Maggie, I met another lawyer who sent me a friend request on Facebook the next day. That's when I noticed his friend Ginna among his Facebook friends, and she was wearing a hiker's backpack. Curious, I clicked on her photo, and amazingly, we had mutual Sherpa friends from climbing to Everest Base Camp in Nepal and had both climbed Mount Kilimanjaro!

I knew very few women who were into "high elevation climbing," and I had to meet this fellow female hiker who had just moved back to Virginia Beach from Colorado. I sent her a friend request, and after a couple of Facebook messages, we met over coffee, and I discovered she was also preparing to lead a climb in Peru. I signed up immediately, as the Machu Picchu trek was on my list of "must-climb mountains." Six months later, I boarded a plane to Cusco, Peru, once the capital of the Inca Empire, to begin what would be one of my favorite hiking adventures ever.

After a couple of nights in our charming hotel near the Plaza de Armas, we were off on an incredible odyssey through the Peruvian jungle and rainforests ending at the celebrated Inca ruins of Machu Picchu, which by the way, reaches nearly 8,000 feet above sea level. Vast green valleys, deep-blue skies, snow-capped mountains, and the occasional white llama literally pranced along the cliffs. I felt like I was hiking inside a postcard.

After a few chilly nights in the tent, we finally made it to Machu Picchu on day four. It was early morning, and the mountain was encased in a white misty cloud, but you could still make out the ancient ruins below—an amazing maze of gray stones stacked along the slopes that, according to archaeologists, was once home to a royal estate or sacred religious site for Inca leaders in the 1400s.

I remember filling my lungs with all that fresh morning air and feeling so incredibly happy that I'd made it! Just six weeks before, I hadn't been sure I would even make the trip. In Colorado, on an assignment for CBN, I had brought my hiking boots along for a practice climb before venturing on the high peaks of Peru. The moment I put my right boot on, I knew something was seriously wrong. Pain shot through my foot. I took my boot off to see what was going on, and there was a small hard knot, about the size of a pea, in the center of my arch.

When I got home, the podiatrist told me it was a plantar fibroma that sometimes develops in the arch of the foot. I was given two options: surgery or a steroid shot—I took the shot and prayed it would literally get me back on my feet!

Unfortunately, I continued to have pain, and the only shoes that didn't hurt were my fur-lined Ugg boots! I had to train for my hike in the muggy spring weather in Uggs! Yuck!

A few weeks before my already paid-for trip, I became very discouraged about my foot and my lack of training. As I sat on the couch, nearly in tears, I said, *"God, I really believed You wanted me to do this climb; why is this happening now?"*

Pull Up Your Boots!

A few minutes later, I checked my email. There was a message from my friend Emily. She said, "Wendy, please read Isaiah 52 today; it's for you." Desperate for any encouragement, I immediately Googled Isaiah 52:1–2 (MSG):

"Wake up, wake up! Pull up your boots, Zion!...Brush off the dust and get to your feet, captive Jerusalem!"

A warm tear ran down my cheek. God was telling me not to worry; I would be pulling on my hiking boots again without pain! Nothing could discourage me now, as I had a word from the Lord! And what a word it was! "Pull up your boots, Wendy!" Yes, the sore, pea-sized bump was still there, but this tiny "mountain" under my foot wasn't going to stop me! After all, didn't Jesus say if you speak to the mountain and tell it to go (even if it's pea-sized), it shall be removed (Mark 11:23)? My attitude now was that God was going to heal me! And even if not fully healed, I was going to crawl my way to Machu Picchu—but I was getting on that plane!

June 7th finally arrived. My flight to Cusco was not until later that evening. As I lay in bed, the sun's rays beckoning me to get up, I heard the Holy Spirit say, "Put on your boots and go for a walk." I was excited and a little bit scared, as I had not been brave enough to put on my boots for about six weeks! As I slipped them on over my hiking socks and put my full weight in the boot, a sense of relief flooded my being. My right foot felt good—not perfect yet, but I didn't have the intense pain I had felt the last time I tried on that boot. I walked for at least an hour before I went home and finished packing for my trip.

The Word of the Lord, sent by my dear friend Emily from England, had become life to me and manifested in my healing! I was now ready for the high peaks of Machu Picchu and a summer that would change everything...

3

Blind Date

"But without faith it is impossible to please Him,
for he who comes to God must believe that He is,
and that He is a rewarder of those who diligently seek Him."

Hebrews 11:6

As we hiked along the Inca Trail, the conversation between two single women naturally turned to dating and men. I confessed to Ginna, "I'm not meeting anyone at church, no one at work, no one on my many plane trips or travels. I don't even wear any rings when I'm on television so there's no confusion about my marital status! It's as if there's a veil over me or something! I feel invisible!" I told her. "I'm truly ready to meet someone, but the only men who are reaching out to me are usually behind bars—literally," I exclaimed. "Apparently *The 700 Club* is popular in prisons, which I'm thankful for, but I just really don't see a future in dating inmates. I don't know where to turn. I don't feel comfortable doing online dating, although I know it works beautifully for many; it's just not for me," I continued. "So...

you know so many people because you grew up in Virginia Beach and because of your profession. How about fixing me up with someone when we get back home?" I asked.

"Sure!" Ginna quickly responded, as if she already had someone in mind...and she did.

Virginia Beach Ocean Front, June 25, 2017

The terrace at the Hilton was crowded when I arrived, as tourists and locals were taking advantage of the late June weather. I was excited. I couldn't remember the last time I had been out with someone of the opposite sex! *Maybe we'll really hit it off,* I thought to myself. *Or maybe, it will just be a fun night at the beach; either way, I'm just happy to be on a real "date,"* I told myself.

The hot summer sun was being perfected by the constant breeze off the ocean when I spotted Ginna and Will talking to a man whom I assumed must be the man they wanted me to meet. Although we had only been back from Peru for two weeks, Ginna and Will had quickly conspired to get the four of us together.

I had seen only one photo of Bill before meeting him, and I liked what I saw, but otherwise, it pretty much felt like a blind date. I didn't know much about him, except that he had gone to Virginia Tech, where Ginna and Will had gone to college, and was in the banking world, a world I knew nothing about.

That evening, wearing a multicolored sun dress with strappy sandals and carrying my new purple llama skin purse I had bought in Peru, I made my way through the sea of people. I was more excited than nervous and, again, just happy to be on a real "date."

The first thing I noticed about Bill was that he was tall and slender, had nice thick brown hair, and ocean blue eyes. The second thing I noticed was his southern accent. "Where are you from?" I asked with my own best southern drawl. "Right here, Virginia Beach," he said with a grin. Although, to me, it sounded decidedly more southern—more like a North Carolina or Georgia twang. I've always been fascinated by accents and definitely have a thing for country boys, so I knew there had to be more to this story.

Because the terrace was so packed, Bill and I had to sit unusually close together on a little wooden bench at one of the outdoor tables, but it didn't feel awkward because Bill seemed so comfortable in his own skin, and that made me feel relaxed as well. Ginna and I couldn't help recounting our recent hiking adventures in Peru, and Will and Bill were good listeners or at least pretended to be! Although it was not "love at first sight," I felt immediately comfortable with him, probably because of his southern drawl and easy conversation.

After a couple of hours of dinner and great conversation, I said goodnight to Ginna and Will, and Bill walked me to the valet stand. While we were waiting for my car, he asked for my phone number. For some strange reason, I put my hand on the side of his face. I immediately thought to myself, *Why am I touching this man's face? I just met him two hours ago!* But for some reason it didn't feel strange. I finally removed my hand from his face, gave him my phone number, and we said goodnight. I didn't see him for another month.

Bill's recollection of our first date is a little different than mine.

Bill writing: In early June 2017, I got a text from my friend Will. Will is many years my junior but reminds me of myself at his age— full of energy, wickedly humorous, and always ready for the next good time. I still have the text he sent me that day on my phone, "You up for meeting someone? I've seen pics. Say yes."

Seemed promising because I do trust Will's taste in women, but I had pretty much given up on dating, at least for a while. I was tired of the stereotypical beach girls I'd grown up with and was finally getting comfortable being single and living on my own again. It had been four years since separating, followed by a painful divorce (is there any other kind?), and I was settling into my new existence. Expecting little, I texted Will back, "We are talking female, right? And human?" One can never be too careful these days, right? Will responded, "Yes. Here you go..." and he attached a link to an interview Wendy had done after writing a book about a tough breakup. I responded back, "Okay, great looking woman, what's the deal?" Will: "She's great. Will let you know more. Will call tomorrow..."

I watched the video link that Will had sent me of Wendy being interviewed and was impressed by her great looks and professionalism. She *sounded* like someone on television! She had obviously been through a tough breakup, but who hadn't? I did take some note of her advice to women about not settling and how she expected to be treated in dating situations. She also was very spiritual and had a strong relationship with God. So now I knew what I was in for! Will kidded me on the phone about boning up on my Bible verses, but I laughed it off and told him I was not going to try to be someone I'm not. I surely wasn't a devout churchgoer at the time and could quote very little Scripture, but I was going to be honest and open-minded.

I told myself the worst that could happen was I would meet an interesting woman, learn something new, or make a new friend. Wendy was certainly very beautiful and accomplished, but I secretly wondered if an obviously very religious woman would fit my lifestyle or have much interest in me. Going into the first "date," I only knew she worked as a television news anchor for the Christian Broadcasting Network (based in Virginia Beach) and had a passion for the outdoors. I was certainly impressed that she had such a successful and unusual career, but her hiking and adventurous spirit attracted me much more than her occupation.

Will contacted me a couple more times once Wendy and our mutual friend, Ginna, returned from Peru to set up a meeting. I was very busy, and the first couple of suggestions didn't work. Eventually, we landed on the Sunday evening at the Hilton. It was a beautiful day, but honestly, I was tired. I had been out late the night before celebrating the seventieth birthday of an old buddy of mine. That affair took place on another friend's hundred-foot motor yacht, where we enjoyed a sunset cruise and party that went well into the night. It was a fun time on a nice summer night on the water to celebrate a great friend. So yeah, I could have used a night off instead of heading out on a Sunday evening, but I didn't want to miss meeting this new woman.

I wasn't nervous driving to the Hilton, perhaps from being a bit tired, and I just reminded myself to have fun and have an open mind.

I was a bit self-conscious since I had just broken my favorite sunglasses and was wearing a pair I use mostly for offshore fishing. They work great for that, but I felt a bit bug-eyed in them. *Oh well, no one will notice*, I told myself. When I arrived, I easily spotted Ginna and Will seated on a bench next to a fire pit. We talked a bit, and soon Wendy arrived. She was wearing a colorful dress and high heels. She was very pretty, but I was not intimidated and found myself at ease right away. I had barely spoken a few words when she looked at me a bit askance and asked, "Where are you from?" The inflection in her voice said, "I've met some real hillbillies before, but which turnip truck did you fall off?" I laughed and tried to explain my slow southern accent and how my northern relatives could barely understand me sometimes. She laughed, and we were off to a good start.

I'm a true Virginia Beach native. My parents moved here in 1954, and my mother still lives in the same house on a saltwater canal near the Chesapeake Bay where I was raised. I had a boat from an early age and would be gone into the bay for most of the day in summer. The water was clear and pristine, and you could always find enough clams or oysters for lunch if you wanted to stay out. My parents had no idea where I was much of the time, but there wasn't much trouble to get into back then.

I guess there was always some country boy in me (which explains the accent). As I got older, I found I enjoyed the mountains and spent many hours hiking and hunting in the Blue Ridge. There was peacefulness and something that just felt right in the mountains. But the beach was my home, and it was not without its charms! In my teens and young adulthood, I surfed, swam, fished, played beach volleyball, studied tanned girls in bikinis, and enjoyed great beach parties. If all this sounds good, let me tell you...ah, shoot, who am I kidding? It was pretty great!

Okay, back to our first date...it was a little difficult trying to explain how my once childhood country "playground" was now surrounded by twenty-story hotels, a concrete boardwalk packed with beachgoers, and bumper-to-bumper traffic! We laughed, and the conversation moved on. *Remember you are who you are,* I reminded myself.

Another recollection early on in our evening was when Wendy asked, "Do you go on many blind dates?" I was a little taken aback because I'd never thought of this meeting as a blind date. To my simple way of thinking, it was just a few friends getting together for an evening at the oceanfront, even if she and I were strangers to start.

I recall sitting very close to Wendy that evening due to the crowd, and I had to put my arm around her on top of the bench in order to turn and somewhat face her for conversation. I silently wondered if that made her uncomfortable, but it seemed natural so we could look at each other to talk. We talked quite a lot about the girls' hike in Peru and some of the other big ones they had done. I had little to add about hiking other than my many times in the Blue Ridge, which seemed kind of like comparing the flattest bunny slope in Virginia to a double black diamond in Aspen. I did have them beat on fishing trips and hours spent on the ocean, so a few fishing and sea stories were in order.

All in all, the conversation flowed easily. We were all comfortable and enjoyed a beautiful evening. I had met someone new, different, and extraordinary without having any upfront expectations. I was kind of proud of myself! She was different from the usual beach girl, and that was nice. I always had a thing for country girls, mountain girls, and adventurous outdoor type women. I can't say it was love at first sight, but I was certainly intrigued enough to want to see Wendy again.

4

Blueberry Picking

"He has made everything beautiful in its time."

Ecclesiastes 3:11

Work, travel, built-in skepticism, and the fact that I wasn't sure we had enough in common allowed me to have a very nonchalant attitude toward seeing Bill again. However, Bill did something right. He pursued me. Let me say that again...*he pursued me.* And he did it in a very laid-back, gentlemanly way and not in a desperate or creepy way. It was more of a polite, respectful, "I'd *actually* like to get to know you" way.

Men, here's a little secret that probably goes against all the advice your buddies have given you since grade school about playing hard to get and not calling a girl for days even if you like her. That advice is simply not true! If you are interested in a girl, you should do your part and let her know. Give her a call to say hello or send her a text to ask how her day is going. Let her know she is on your mind. Even if she is not that interested in the beginning (she may have other things she is dealing with and may not be quite ready to jump into a relationship), your gentlemanly pursuit of her will not go unnoticed. Eventually, if it's meant to be, these gestures will open up her heart. If it's not meant to be, what harm have you done other than let someone else know that they are special enough for you to be thinking of them? Women were designed to be won over, as I wrote about at length in my prior book, *You Are a Prize to Be Won, Don't Settle for Less than God's Best*. To all the men out there: How can you win the prize if you don't pursue it?

And that's exactly what happened to me. Every few days, Bill would send me a sweet text asking about my day or take time to call and chat. It made me stop and pay a little more attention to him as a potential boyfriend. Then, about a month after our initial meeting, Ginna and I met up with Will and Bill again. It was a Wednesday night in late July at an event at the Virginia Beach Town Center called "Why Not Wednesdays," which was honestly my state of mind. *Why not?* I had nothing to lose, and Bill had asked me to meet, so again, *why not?* We had fun chatting with the guys and listening to music, but Bill and I did not make any immediate plans to see each other again. There was one strange "coincidence" that came out of our Wednesday meet-up, though. Somehow in conversation, Bill mentioned that he was going hunting in Canada that October. I told him I was also headed to Canada in October. "Which province?" I asked him.

"Saskatchewan," Bill said. "Me too!" I excitedly responded.

"Where *exactly* in Saskatchewan?" I continued, more curious than ever.

"We'll fly into Saskatoon, and then we'll travel by truck to the prairies where we go duck hunting," Bill told me. I was simply astounded because I was also going to Saskatoon but not to hunt. I was honored to be the keynote speaker at one of the largest Christian women's conferences in Western Canada. I thought to myself, *What are the chances of this?* Canada is a huge country, and we're both going to the same town in the same province in the same month. I'm a sucker for signs, and this was an absolute doozie. After all, I had never even heard of Saskatoon until I was invited to speak there, and now this guy I had just met told me he goes there almost every fall to hunt. I told the Lord this "sign" was good, but I would need much more than this before I'd let my heart believe again.

It wouldn't be long before we saw each other again. The following Saturday morning, while I was still lying in bed contemplating my day, my phone rang. It was Bill. He asked me if I wanted to go blueberry picking in Pungo, a rural area near Virginia Beach. Well, who doesn't want to go blueberry picking? As you can imagine, I jumped out of bed and got ready as fast as I could.

Women, don't we just love a man with a plan—a man who has come up with a great date idea and doesn't have to ask us, "So what do you want to do?"? Not that we can't come up with some fun date ideas as well, but it's refreshing when we don't have to. This is especially true when you first start going out with someone new. For me, it shows what type of person you are spending time with. Is he a leader or a follower? Is he focused only on his own interests, or is he concerned about me and what I may consider a fun and exciting date? Whether he knew it or not, Bill was certainly doing all the right things.

It was now late July, and there were just enough blueberries left on the bushes to fill a couple of small buckets to take home. Once again, the conversation was fun and easy as we talked, flirted, and looked for the few choice berries that remained. On our drive back to my office, where I had parked my car, we found ourselves following a car with a Canadian license plate. The plate was adorned with a maple leaf, which is the national symbol of Canada. I started thinking again about the apparent "coincidence" and decided to Google the meaning of the maple leaf. What I found was interesting, to say the least. "The maple leaf is an ancient symbol of love, most notably in China and Japan. Like the sweet sap from its tree, which ultimately produces maple syrup, maple leaves represent the sweetness and wonder of love in daily life" ("12 Unique Symbols of Love in Art History," invaluable.com).

Could it be? I thought to myself. It was still too soon to know, but when we said our goodbyes next to his white Tacoma pick-up truck, I remember thinking I wanted Bill to feel the love of Jesus in my hug. By then, I knew he had been through a lot with his divorce and, like all of us, was someone Jesus wanted to heal and bless. So I said a silent prayer, gave him my best bear hug, and got in my car and drove off. I didn't know it quite then, but that day my summer had just taken an exciting turn, and the best was yet to come.

Chapter 4: Blueberry Picking

Bill's Thoughts on That Day...

Saying I had an actual plan might be giving me too much credit! I did have an idea and an activity the right woman might enjoy. I guess I'm a hunter-gatherer at heart and just can't get away from it. Any activity is better if there's a chance I can get some food out of it! So I gave Wendy a call mid-morning, and as I recall, she wasn't that keen on getting together until I mentioned the idea of picking fruit! So we agreed to meet at CBN, where she worked, and I would drive to the field from there.

Wendy looked very cute and relaxed in a pair of shorts and a cool tank top she got at a restaurant in Florida. It said "Red Fish, Blue Fish" on it, which of course suited my taste very well. We had a short ride to get more acquainted before arriving at the field. It was indeed slim pickings, but we found enough berries to make us happy as we talked and flirted the time away. Afterward, we stopped by a produce stand and bought some vegetables and prolonged our day. Later in our dating life, Wendy told me at that stand, I touched her arm in some way that made her feel warm and fuzzy. Although I only vaguely remembered doing so, it was certainly an impulsive thing, and I had no real intentions. But she definitely remembered! The thing is, most guys don't really have deep thoughts at this stage (if rarely ever!). We just sort of go with the flow and don't overthink much. Women tend to put more stock in some of our actions than we expect. Men are really quite simple. We probably just go along, not thinking about much most of the time!

In any event, we had another twenty-minute ride back to CBN, and our conversation continued. Somewhere along the way, we saw the car with the Canadian maple leaf license, which opened up our conversation of Canada again. It did seem unusual that both of us would be going to such a random (often below zero) remote place at almost the same time. I've been going up there for over twenty years to hunt and love the people, the open land, and the memorable waterfowl hunts. She would be arriving just a few days after I left. I remember thinking how cool it would have been if our paths crossed there, but I wasn't sure she'd be impressed with the open prairie where we hunt. And honestly, there's not much else to do up there in October! Finally, we arrived back at CBN and got out of my truck to say our goodbyes. Wendy gave me a prolonged hug that I remember felt really good. I didn't even try to kiss her, even though it felt like the time was right. I knew or hoped at least that there would be plenty of time for that later. I was in no hurry.

5

A Girl's Gotta Eat

"The people who give you their food give you their heart."

—Caser Chavez

They say a good meal is the best way to a man's heart, but one taste of Bill's cooking and I was nearly in love.

Not long after our blueberry picking date, Bill invited me over to his place for dinner. I liked his manly style: hardwood floors, a wood-burning fireplace with a deer head over the mantle, and gorgeous granite kitchen countertops with dangling pendant lights—the quintessential bachelor pad. I also quickly discovered that Bill was a skilled and passionate fisherman with a freezer full of every kind of fish you can imagine, from flounder and sea bass to more exotic varieties, including sheepshead and tautog. And he had caught it all in the deep waters off the Virginia Beach coast.

I've always loved fish. It's delicious, healthy, high in protein, and low in calories. That night, as I sat at his kitchen counter, I watched intently as he prepared the flounder filets in a big iron skillet with butter and a spicy cajun seasoning. He added some steamed asparagus, wild rice, and a colorful salad to the meal as well. It was a work of art! I actually took a picture because it was so pretty. I was impressed with Bill's ease in the kitchen, something I was still working on. The first bite was heavenly. I honestly thought flounder had to be fried to taste good, but this, and I'm not exaggerating, was truly the best flounder I had ever tasted.

After dinner, we took a walk on the beach under a full moon. I tried to show off a bit by doing cartwheels on the sand. Once a cheerleader, always a cheerleader! Bill showed off, too, by taking me by his buddy's waterfront mansion. His friend wasn't home, but we still enjoyed walking around his pool and imagining how the superrich live. It was a perfect evening.

"The Talk"

During one of our first few dates, Bill and I had what I like to call "the talk." This was when I explained to him that I was waiting until marriage for sex. Bill really didn't seem surprised. He clearly understood and respected me, and that made me like him even more. After having my heart broken way too many times in my twenties, I made the decision that I would "save" myself for marriage. At age twenty-nine, I gave my life to Christ, so this decision was as much to protect my heart and emotional state as it was to honor God. I never wanted to feel that pain and shame again that I'd experienced when I was younger after giving myself away to someone who didn't value me. And I finally understood why God asks us to wait—not to keep us from pleasure but to protect us from pain. Of course, when you're physically attracted to someone, and Bill and I were very much so, it's not easy to wait. With God's grace, though, all things are possible!

The Breakup

The summer of 2017 flew by with lots more flounder dinners, fishing in the Chesapeake Bay, evening boat rides to take in the fiery orange sunsets, and romantic walks on the beach. I liked Bill—a lot— but I wasn't sure if this had just been a fun summer romance or if we were built to go the distance, as in marriage. My biggest concern was whether we were spiritually compatible. We went to church together and prayed together, but I was worried that my devotion to God would be too much for him. In Bill's defense, though, he had never given me any indication to justify my concern. Still, I let my anxieties and insecurities get the best of me, and I panicked!

Then, at the end of a beautiful summer, I broke up with Bill! Ugggh! I really hate reliving this because it was quite painful, and I was the one self-inflicting this pain on both of us!

We were sitting on the beach watching the waves roll in when I told Bill I thought we should stop seeing each other. I was literally sobbing as Bill sat stoically trying to make sense of it all. As we stood at our cars to say goodbye, I was still crying, and he was still mainly silent and looking confused. Bill was certainly not the type of person to "beg" for another chance or apologize. After all, he had done nothing wrong, so why would he apologize? Finally, we hugged goodbye, got in our cars, and drove in opposite directions.

Looking back, I see that fear was taking over. Fear of wasting precious time continuing to date Bill if he wasn't the one. After all, I was almost fifty-three and didn't feel I had any more time to lose. But fear is not from God. Instead, I should have been trusting God and letting Him lead. Earlier that day, before meeting Bill, I saw a sign on a white van outside the coffee shop where I was sitting with friends. It read, "Don't Panic." I should have paid more attention, as, in retrospect, I believe God was speaking to me. Yes, that's how God often talks to me—through vanity plates and things written on vans—but I ignored the message and hurt someone I cared way more deeply for than I even realized.

It was a Thursday night, and, as you can imagine, my weekend was miserable and seemed to drag on forever.

Thankfully, God had a different plan. That Sunday, a friend I hadn't heard from in a while sent me an email that simply said, "I had a word from God that you need this," and it was a link to the song "Take Me Home, Country Roads" by John Denver. I love that song, and being from West Virginia, it holds a special place in my heart, but I dismissed the email as nothing important. Then, my friend sent me the backstory to the song by John Denver. Apparently, according to my friend, but I couldn't confirm this, Denver penned the song after an argument with his love, and somehow it helped patch up the relationship. I have no idea if that's true. All I know is that God was speaking to me, saying, "Ummm...you missed it—I never told you to break up with him, and you should get back together."

CHAPTER 5: A GIRL'S GOTTA EAT

VA Tech vs. WVU

Turns out that Sunday night, Virginia Tech (where Bill went to college) and WVU (where I went to college) were playing football in a highly anticipated match-up. It was Labor Day weekend, and I knew Bill would be watching. Virginia Tech ended up beating WVU 31–24 that Sunday night in a pretty exciting game. I sent Bill a text to congratulate him on the win. He texted back, saying, "Thanks. Didn't we have a bet on this game?" I didn't remember if we did or not, but I was thankful he was being playful after what had just transpired a few days ago. I said, "Sure—you name it." He said, "I want you to take me hiking at Old Rag." I said, "Done." And just like that, we were back on.

The very next weekend, we summited Old Rag—my favorite mountain in Virginia's Shenandoah National Park—a part of the Blue Ridge Mountains. Old Rag would be very significant later on for Bill and me, but that story later. Turns out Bill was a fantastic hiker, and we kept perfect pace together the three hours up the mountain and the two and a half hours down. I was reminded of what Bill said to me when we first met, "I feel like I'm supposed to show you my world (boats, fishing, hunting) and you're supposed to show me your world (God, church, and hiking)."

During the four-hour drive home, we sang out loud songs playing on the radio—or songs I pulled up on my iPhone. And as fate would have it, the very last song we sang (at the top of our lungs) was "Take Me Home, Country Roads" by John Denver. As we pulled back into my parking space at my condo, the song ended as if on cue, "Take me home, down country roads."

Bill's Side of the Story

So our first dinner date at my house was totally spontaneous, and truthfully, I was playing defense. It was a very hot, humid August day, and I had been rebuilding the dock at my parent's house. I spent the day in and out of the salt water and mud and was covered in sweat, sawdust, and dirt and had a few cuts and bruises from hammering, drilling, and hauling lumber all day. I was tired and not very presentable. But my new love interest texted me in the late afternoon, asking if I could join her for some sun and fun on the beach. I looked like the creature from the Black Lagoon and desperately needed a shower before I interacted with anyone. Fortunately, I had been fishing a few days earlier and had some nice flounder filets in the cooler (pro tip: fresh fish keeps better packed in ice than sitting in the refrigerator for a few days), so I devised a quick plan. I told Wendy I would make her dinner if she wanted to come over but to give me time for a shower first. It took a little convincing, but she agreed. I was fired up for us to get together, and the cooking part came together perfectly.

Bill on the "Breakup"

As for the end-of-summer breakup, I was confused but more disappointed. I knew I hadn't done anything wrong, but I didn't share her deep spirituality, so I reasoned maybe it just wasn't meant to be. I just wished we'd had more of a chance. I wrote her a long letter, mostly just expressing disappointment for the fact that we didn't get much time to really know each other or see where it would go. I never sent it. I think it was Labor Day weekend, and the weekend went by quietly and quickly. Prior to the breakup, we had planned to get together for the VT/WVU football game with Ginna and some of my friends. As it turned out, I watched the game at those same friends' house with some fellow Hokies and our host's wife, who was a Mountaineer. She didn't get to burn her couch that night! (A WVU tradition after home game wins.)

After the game, I headed back to my condo at the beach and crawled into bed. I was happy to get Wendy's text congratulating me on the win. I responded, and we ended up having a midnight phone conversation. Neither one of us mentioned the breakup, and I was just happy to have an easy conversation with her. But I did seize the opportunity! I figured she might not remember if we bet on the game or not. So even though there was truly no bet, I took a chance, said there was, and she took the bait by asking what I wanted as the winner. I asked for a hiking trip, and well, you know the rest.

6

Lean Not

"Trust in the Lord with all your heart and lean not on your
own understanding; In all your ways acknowledge Him,
and He will direct your paths."

Proverbs 3:5–6

Although Bill and I had survived the mini-breakup and were
talking and seeing each other again, my heart was still wavering.
I wanted to know! Was he the man I would be waking up with
and going to sleep with for the rest of my life? The biological clock
had probably already timed out, but I didn't want to waste another
second of my life going in a direction that wasn't the one God had
for me. It was my fifty-third birthday, and I had just picked up my
uncle's wife, Tish (hard for me to call her my aunt because we're
the same age), at Norfolk International Airport. She was waving a
nicely wrapped gift in her hand as she smiled and walked toward
me on the tarmac. She had remembered it was my birthday. We
were on our way to see her then fourteen-year-old daughter Carly

play in a tennis tournament that, fortunately for me, was happening here in Virginia Beach. After the match, which Carly won, we were in my car chatting about Bill and my upcoming birthday dinner date later that evening. I told them I really liked Bill a lot but still wasn't sure if he was the one.

Lean Not

Then, suddenly, as if on cue, the vanity plate of a car right in front of us grabbed my attention—*lean not*! It seemed to be almost screaming at me. "Look at that vanity plate, guys! Lean Not!" I screamed back. I immediately knew it was a reference to the often-quoted scripture from Proverbs 3:5, "*Trust in the Lord with all your heart and lean not on your own understanding.*" God was clearly talking to me as He'd done many times before through vanity plates, and this time the message was unmistakably clear: *Stop trying to figure it all out—you don't have to know how this story ends yet. I'm in charge—not you!* Suddenly, a peace came over me. God wanted me to enjoy the journey and let Him take the wheel. I could sit back and enjoy being courted, enjoy being taken out to dinner for my birthday, and enjoy a man's attention without having to know immediately if I was going to marry him. What a concept! I was now looking forward to my dinner date with Bill, girded with a new mindset that God was in control and I could just relax and enjoy the ride.

That night we dined on the water at one of my favorite restaurants in Virginia Beach, The Porch on Long Creek, although at that time, it was called One Fish-Two Fish. The sunset was spectacular that night—dark pink, purple, and neon coral painted across the horizon, and we had a perfect waterside table to watch the boats go by and take it all in. I almost missed the sunset completely because I was running late after struggling to put false eyelashes on (which I never wear), but I wanted to look extra glam for my birthday. Bill finally noticed them about halfway through the evening and was very appreciative of the effort but said they probably weren't necessary. I agreed. The warm mid-September air wrapped around us like a big hug, and Bill and I laughed the night away. It was truly a birthday celebration to remember.

The Light Bulb Comes On

Later that month, my younger brother Pete, an attorney who lives in Charlottesville, Virginia, was in town for a lawyer's meeting. We met for dinner in downtown Norfolk so we could catch up. It had been a while since we'd seen each other, and we had a lot to talk about. Pete had not yet met Bill and wanted to learn more about him, so I got out my cell phone and started going through all the photos of Bill and me from the last few months, starting with our very first date in late June to the many days on his boat—fishing for flounder in the Chesapeake Bay or just cruising for fun—to pictures of us hiking my beloved Old Rag Mountain and finally my birthday celebration two weeks ago. As I shared the stories behind each photo with Pete, it was as if a lightbulb was slowly coming on in my heart. By the time I had finished the picture show and was telling Pete what a kind, caring, fun, and handsome guy Bill was, the lightbulb was all the way on, and it was really bright! I told my brother, "I have to go! I have to go see Bill." It was Wednesday, September 27th, 2017, and that's when I knew I was in love with Bill Susewind. Don't worry—I didn't tell Bill yet. That would come later.

7

Pittsburgh

Go Steelers!

It was now nearly Thanksgiving, and Bill and I were officially an item—but are you really "official" if you haven't posted it and declared it on Facebook? Ha, that would come soon enough. For now, though, it was time for Bill to meet the family and vice versa.

My younger sister Nancy, her husband, John, and daughter, Sydney, live just outside of Pittsburgh and, for years, have hosted Thanksgiving celebrations at their lovely and spacious home. As the only single sibling out of five, I would normally fly in on Thanksgiving Day just as the turkey was being taken out of the oven. It was perfect, and I wasn't required to do anything but show up, eat, and enjoy.

This time would be different. I was bringing my boyfriend, Bill. I loved how musical that sounded, "Boyfriend Bill." I was excited and a little nervous, as this was the first time in years I had brought anyone of the opposite sex home to meet the family, but I had a feeling they were going to like him as much as I did.

When we arrived at Nancy's home, my nieces and nephews were already gathered in the kitchen. They ranged in age from about five to seventeen. I'll never forget the look on their faces. They could not take their eyes off Bill and me. They were so accustomed to seeing Aunt Wendy flying solo during the holidays and other times, for that matter, they didn't know what to make of this tall, handsome bearded man standing beside her. Their wide-eyed expressions said it all, "Is this our future uncle? Is he just a friend? Why is Aunt Wendy standing so close to him?" It was hilarious because they literally just kept staring and smiling. Even now, we still have a good laugh when we talk about their reaction.

Bill is one of those fortunate people who is very comfortable in his own skin and can handle almost any personality, including my mother, Georgia. When he met my mom for the first time, she was sitting on a bar stool with her feet propped up on another bar stool wearing socks that said on the bottom, "Bring me wine." Bill sauntered over to her and squeezed her feet and said hello. I think my mom was smitten with him in that moment.

The weekend flew by with lots of eating, hiking in the nearby hills around my sister's home, and a memorable night at the top of Pittsburgh's famous Mount Washington, known for its stunning panoramic city views, especially at night. From that vantage point, you not only see the twinkling lights from downtown but the three rivers that converge in "The Steel City," the Monongahela, the Allegheny, and the Ohio Rivers. That night, about twenty-five members of my family got all dressed up and met at one of the more glamorous restaurants on Mount Washington. The beautiful chandeliers and floor-to-ceiling windows showcasing the sparkling lights from the city below created an unforgettable ambiance for celebration and, yes, romance. It was the Saturday after Thanksgiving, and we were toasting my uncle Truman and his wife Tish's wedding anniversary as we often do during Thanksgiving weekend, but also, it felt very much like a party to welcome Bill to the family, and he was definitely the star of the show that weekend.

We took so many fun photos that night—one of which would become our "Facebook official" picture that caused quite an avalanche of congratulations and as many questions from both his friends and mine. I was wearing a red sleeveless dress and long sparkling earrings, and Bill looked so handsome in his navy blue "date night" shirt I had helped him pick out for the weekend. As I hit the "share" button on Facebook, I had a feeling everything was about to change, but I was ready for change and ready as I'd ever be to introduce "Boyfriend Bill" to my world.

The next night would also be a first for Bill and me. And my first NFL game! It was a cold Sunday night, but we were bundled up and ready to see the Pittsburgh Steelers beat the Green Bay Packers. To say that Steeler fans are passionate about their team would be a huge understatement. There's a reason they call themselves "Steeler Nation," and I was about to find out. My brother-in-law John is probably one of their biggest fans and rarely misses a game. He took us to a sort of "Steeler Initiation" pre-game party where we ate from the longest sub sandwich I'd ever seen and huddled around burning trash cans to stay warm. Anyone who braves these cold Pittsburgh nights to cheer on their team deserves to be part of "Steeler Nation," and tonight, Bill and I were privileged to be "adopted" into the Steeler family. Finally, it was time to find our seats in the stadium. John had made sure we had our yellow "terrible towels" to wave. The Steelers' colors are black and gold, and it's a tradition at Steeler games to wave the yellow "terrible towel" in the air when you're cheering them on.

At one point during the night, I looked over at Bill, and he was smiling, but his eyes were glistening with tears. I asked him what was going on, and he said, "It's been a long time since I've been this happy." I was starting to realize that Bill wasn't just my answer to prayer. I was his answer to prayer. Our prayers were also answered for the Steelers that night as Placekicker Chris Boswell kicked a career-long fifty-three-yard field goal as time expired to give the Steelers a 31–28 victory over the Packers. I wonder if God had a hidden meaning in this for me, as I was fifty-three and feeling like my time to meet someone was about to "expire"—but just like God pulled it out for the Steelers in the last second, He was doing the same for me. God is seldom early, but He's never late.

By the end of that weekend, my seventeen-year-old niece Madison gave me her approval of Bill as did my other niece, Kelly Anne, a true romantic at heart, who, at the tender age of eight, was more than ready to call him Uncle Bill.

Truth be told, that weekend sort of sealed the deal in my heart as well. My family's opinion is very important to me, and the fact that they all really liked him (as opposed to the last guy I brought home) made me even more confident that Bill could be "the one."

8

Bill's Story

"Weeping may endure for a night, But joy comes in the morning."

Psalm 30:5

I'm divorced. It's a fact I'm not proud of. I will forever be sorry that it's a part of my history. I'm ashamed of some of my behavior before, during, and after the fact. I wish I could undo the fighting, emotional stress, and pain we both endured. I would not wish a divorce on anyone. It's devastating emotionally and is truly exhausting. I encourage those with marital difficulties to communicate better and try hard to work things out. I didn't do a good job of that. I suppose a certain amount of guilt will always remain, but in the big picture, I had to let it go to survive and prosper. Clinging to the past doesn't allow us to move forward. And forward is where you must go in that situation. Forgiveness can relieve you of some burden. There is hope. Have faith that you will be okay. You just might have to live through some hell to get there.

Men Have Feelings Too

It's hard to describe the feelings I experienced. Perhaps more so as a man, since we aren't really wired to deal with feelings (yes, we do have some feelings, ladies, despite our tough exteriors)! I fancy myself to be a decent writer, but I'm much more qualified to describe to you the thrill of a white marlin coming to your bait behind the boat, the awe of a flock of ducks circling your decoys during a duck hunt, or the beauty of a deer appearing in the early morning light while watching quietly from my tree stand than I am qualified to describe feelings. But I'll give it a try in hopes it may help someone going through something similar.

You Reap What You Sow in Marriage

I did many things wrong along the way, neglecting important things that feed a marriage. I didn't communicate when I was struggling. I didn't put much work into my marriage, and the marriage suffered. You reap what you sow. I was told by a marriage counselor we visited that we were very good at taking care of business but very bad at taking care of each other. We paid our bills on time and met all of our responsibilities but put little effort into each other. I was not romantic. I did not do many of the little things that a woman wants from her husband. I complained a lot, even when there was nothing to complain about. Most of all, I didn't put my wife first. Humans (not just women) want to be appreciated. Women, in particular, want to be considered first before other options. They simply want to know you love them and want to be with them above all else, which can be hard during deer season. Constantly planning your next hunting or fishing trip without any consideration to their needs or desires leads to feelings of unimportance and frustration. An encouraging spouse is certainly happy for you to pursue your passions, but not when it takes all your resources and energy so there is none left to spend on them. And certainly, don't make them last on the list.

In any long-term relationship, lives become entwined in every way and much more deeply than you realize. Families become each other's in-laws. Children, friends, neighbors, and relatives all come to know you and your spouse as a unit. You may own a home together, have a joint checking account or credit card, have kids or dogs, and use the same cell phone provider or email account. Your car insurance is from the same provider, and you have a family budget. You're invited to parties or weddings and go to concerts as a couple, and you may vacation with other couples. You learn the other's interests, thought processes, views of politics and the world, likes and dislikes, how to prepare the food they like, and which knife your spouse thinks should be used for what purpose in the kitchen!

You take each other to work when the car's in the shop; you exercise together, eat together, and sleep together. You work together to maintain your house, yard, cars, and toys, and you try to save some money. You talk about the future. You may share the same hobbies, and you know the little things that make your spouse happy. You also know what upsets them and how far to go with a joke. (I've always had a problem with that one!) But there is comfort in this association and knowledge of one another. Your spouse is always there for you and is on your side. Being settled feels good, especially if you're older. You are content to relax together, fix some dinner, and pet the dog on Friday night. I think they call it "adulting" these days.

Separated or divorced, you lose those things. Your safety net is gone, and you feel like you're free-falling sometimes. It's very uncomfortable. Now you're unraveling all those things that were so intertwined. You haven't lived until you've tried to call Verizon to separate your cell phone bills! But your new-found freedom can be exciting, and the world filled with new possibilities. I vacillated between feelings of excitement and lonely Sunday nights when the weekend was over. You and the ex will talk and text because you're still not sure how to do this. It's more complicated with kids or dogs. Some of the talks will be supportive and productive and leave you feeling okay. Others will tear you apart and make you miserable. It's all part of the process. Going out on your own will be strange at first, as the world feels very foreign, unfamiliar, and uncomfortable. There are times when you think people are looking at you or can just see that you are divorced and on your own. You are no longer part of that unit I mentioned above, and that unit gave you more comfort than you once believed.

Take Your Time

Men try to be macho and ignore any feeling of loneliness or even responsibility for their circumstances. We try to "get back on the horse" as soon as possible because nothing replaces a soured relationship quite like several more! Men should slow down and take their time to process their situation, give themselves time to get used to the new normal, and be truly ready for a relationship when one comes along (assuming you want another meaningful relationship). I know a few dedicated bachelors and some bachelorettes who are perfectly happy on their own or with more casual relationships. There's nothing wrong with that if it's what you want. That said, if you're looking or bored, it is time to get out there and have some fun! Sitting at home stewing is not a healthy thing either. Just relax, go with the flow, enjoy what comes your way, and keep the ego in check. Everyone experiences divorce (or a breakup) in their own way. I took comfort in some relationship bloggers I found online who insisted wherever you are now is exactly where you are supposed to be, and it is part of your unique journey.

The belief that God has a plan for you can give you some comfort in the dark times.

Back in the day, my parents enjoyed a humorist named Erma Bombeck, who wrote a popular newspaper column and many books about suburban home life from the 1960s to the 1990s. One of the little gems we had on the coffee table when I was a kid was a book entitled *The Grass Is Always Greener, Over the Septic Tank*. I couldn't tell you anything about the book, but the title appeals to my sense of humor and could be pretty adept at describing the dating situation of a divorcé. The world is indeed full of princes and princesses, but there are definitely a lot of frogs to kiss too. I was what the world calls middle-aged when I got divorced but felt like I was thirty-five. At my chronological age, people have baggage. Most single folks in their fifties have been through some relationships, both good and bad. Many are divorced (some a few times); many have children or elderly parents to care for; some have siblings they don't get along with, pets that bite or potty in the house, crazy families, or just unique behaviors. We are all crazy in some ways; it's just a matter of how much crazy you can put up with!

I Wanted Something Different

I had an interesting first date with a very attractive young lady who confessed early on she had been married and divorced three times. She told me she made poor choices in men. She also told me on the second marriage she never even took her belongings out of storage! Apparently, she saw that end coming. Another very nice woman absolutely refused to tell me how old she was (no, I didn't ask specifically, but you generally try to figure these things out). One time, she left her driver's license on the countertop and was quite upset with herself, as I may have seen it. I did but couldn't see the numbers without my reading glasses! Another still ran a business with her ex-husband and had to immediately take his phone calls at any time, day or night, no matter what, or incur his wrath. I never tried online dating but went back to the traditional methods of meeting women—the gym or parties and social gatherings. I'm very social and have lots of friends and had many opportunities to mingle. It was not hard to meet people or strike up conversations or get invited to gatherings. There were plenty of eligible women. One thing I did notice—there was a core group of guys and gals who attended every gathering. I knew a few of them from my early single days, met their friends, and observed their behaviors. I live in a pretty populated city, but it's a small town. In that clique everyone knew everyone, their past history, and their business. I tried, but I couldn't get comfortable with that group. I could just see myself dating one of the available ones and her reporting back to the group immediately and in great detail! Maybe I was paranoid or just not very confident in myself, but I just couldn't get involved. I did meet some very nice and interesting women, but none of them piqued my interest. It wasn't them. I just wasn't ready.

Bed Bath & Beyond is no place for a man. As I mentioned, being divorced can thrust you into some unfamiliar and uncomfortable positions. Once separated from my wife, I moved into a condo I had bought in my twenties that was formerly our rental property. For the first year, I slept on a mattress and box spring on the floor. I may have suffered from a bit of depression during that time. Once it became official that I would be on my own for good, I knew it was time to buy some furniture, be more comfortable, and perhaps get better rest (divorce is not good for getting good rest, although it's pretty good for losing weight). I hit a great sale and got a nice bedroom set with a king bed and a new couch. I was feeling pretty good about it all when I realized I needed sheets and other accouterments for the bed. I headed over to Bed Bath & Beyond after work one night to get set up. It was then I realized I knew nothing about bedding. My mother had probably set me up with my first set of sheets after college, and my ex had done the rest for our time together. I quickly found out this was not like going to the tackle store, where I knew my way around. I pondered thread counts, pillow materials, comforters versus quilts, blankets, throw pillows, pillowcases, and what the heck is a duvet? I narrowly averted a panic attack, swallowed all my pride, and called my ex. To her credit, she walked me through some options, and after an inordinate amount of time, I got some good and comfortable bedding! Decent bedding is not cheap, by the way, but it does make sleeping more comfortable!

I spent a few years as a single guy living in the condo near the Virginia Beach oceanfront. I enjoyed biking on the boardwalk in the mornings and exercising. I was close to restaurants and entertainment but spent most of my summertime on the boat fishing and boat riding. I really wanted someone special to enjoy it with me, but that didn't happen. Falls and winters were spent hunting. I got used to being on my own and being alone, but it took a while to get comfortable with it. I still lacked complete confidence in myself. I spent many evenings alone by the fire or watching TV with the dogs. It was just easier that way. I always felt I would remarry but didn't know when or how it might happen. I spent some time with an old girlfriend, but we were better as friends than we were as a couple (perhaps explaining why she was an old girlfriend!). The women I met just weren't what I was looking for; they either came on way too strong or were quite aloof. There was too much partying, and I saw people my age who just lived to make it to the next party and drink more. It was disillusioning and depressing. My ex-wife and I continued a unique arrangement where we shared custody of our two dogs, one week on and one week off. We tried to cover each other if one was going out of town or needed consideration for some activity. We went through periods where we got along and others where we didn't. It sometimes led to great frustration and kept the pain of our divorce near the surface for longer than it should have. I was okay, but not really happy, and dealing with a lot of frustration. I had some good times but never felt truly fulfilled. I began to wonder if I would ever feel better again.

A Breakthrough Prayer

One dark evening my frustration came to a head. Something had led me to be stressed and upset, and I specifically remember standing in my walk-in closet, throwing my arms in the air, and screaming out to the Lord. I don't remember my exact words, but I begged God for relief from my frustration and pain. I explained my case in detail and that despite my sins, I wanted a second chance, a new beginning, and although I knew I didn't deserve anything, I didn't feel I deserved to be tortured like this. I asked to be forgiven. Here I was, a self-proclaimed Christian who never went to church, only said the occasional prayer when a big fish was on the line, and was asking for forgiveness! What had just come over me? I didn't really know, but the event was obviously memorable. Had I been saved without even knowing it? After that I did things a little differently. I let some of the frustration go and looked more on the bright side. I still had a good job, a home in a cool place, some money in the bank, two great dogs I loved, a boat, tons of friends, and many fishing and hunting trips, and my parents were alive and healthy in their old age. I gave up worrying about dates or finding the perfect woman. At this point, I had been officially divorced for about a year but separated and living on my own for nearly three years. Should she never appear, I'd be fine on my own. A few months later, I met a beautiful dark-haired woman through some mutual friends who changed everything!

Forget about Your Type

Here's some great advice for those seeking a relationship—forget about your "type." We all have a type of guy or girl we are attracted to. For me it was the beach girl, thin, blonde, tanned, and athletic. Wendy grew up attracted to the tall, dark, and handsome Italian type. So how does it work if I'm attracted to thin, blonde beach girls, and she likes Italian men? How did we find a happy marriage when she is a curvy brunette and I'm a thin guy with brown hair? The key is to have an open mind. Earlier in the book, I wrote about meeting with Wendy with no expectations and an open mind. She did the same. We hit it off and are now happily married. We are both very attracted to each other. Don't pigeonhole yourself into only looking for your "type"! There are so many interesting people out there to meet that you may be overlooking. Relax, and don't worry about your type. Let God lead you.

Know Your Worth

Everyone should know their worth and not accept less than they deserve. Your gender doesn't matter. My mother once told me she thought one of my old girlfriends treated me like a toy. She played with me when she wanted to but put me back on a shelf otherwise. If she saw this, why didn't I? The bottom line is you deserve the best for yourself, whoever you are. My wife wrote an impactful book, *You Are a Prize to Be Won, Don't Settle for Less than God's Best*, that shares the female perspective on seeking God to know your value, how to heal from heartbreak, and practical tips on how to meet the one God has prepared for you. Please buy several copies.

Show Me Your World

Wendy always said she was not on the five-year plan. Truthfully, I wasn't either. We were both of the dreaded "middle age," and if it was right, there was no reason to wait and date for years before committing. That may be an advantage of being a bit older—you know more of what you want and don't waste time. But was I afraid? Yes, of trusting my own judgment initially and the possibility of my own behavior messing it up along the way! When we first met, I told her, "I believe I'm supposed to show you my world, and you're supposed to show me your world." I still believe that is true. I showed her fresh fish for dinner, water sports, boating, nice sunsets, and the beauty of the coast we live on. Wendy showed me faith in action and a love of God and expanded my spirituality. She also showed me her world of travel.

Wendy was invited to attend a wedding for a colleague who was from Norway. The wedding would be held there in the seaside city of Bergen. Wendy wanted to go and asked if I wanted to come. We'd go to the wedding, do some sightseeing, enjoy the food, and go hiking. I'd never been to Europe and don't love to fly, but I had a beautiful woman asking me to come along for a grand adventure in a place I never would have seen on my own. I was keeping that open mind I talked about and knew I needed to expand my horizons and do some things differently than I had thus far in life. It didn't take me long to say yes! By now our relationship had become more serious, and we were shifting our thinking to the possibility of the longer term. There were no commitments at this point, but neither of us was on the five-year plan either. We enjoyed a great wedding celebration, met some very nice Norwegians, endured some good-natured prodding from some of the guests (when will you guys be getting engaged?), great seafood, train rides, and beautiful scenery in the fiords. But I was still skeptical, not of Wendy but of myself. I wondered if I could trust my own judgment in choosing another partner. Could I do the things necessary to make it work? Could I be 100 percent committed and work to make a marriage succeed where I failed once before? Maybe I just wasn't cut out for marriage. Wendy could sense it, and we had a sharp conversation one night over there where she theorized that perhaps we had seen enough of each other's lives, and that was all that was intended. I didn't want to lose her and took notice. I think Wendy was working on her own fears at that time. She had been heartbroken before and didn't want to invest emotionally in someone who was just being casual or noncommittal. I noticed as we dated that Wendy could roll with almost any punches and have a good time, but she spooked easily at any hint that I might be less than committed. "I love you, but..." was something she never wanted to hear again. We really couldn't blame each other; it was just a product of where we were in life and our experiences. In the end, Norway was a wonderful experience and brought us closer and with a better understanding of one another. I wonder what those hecklers at the wedding would think if they could see us now!

The Best Is Yet to Come

So Wendy and I each had our concerns and worries about relationships and commitment. She didn't want to be built up only to be let down again, and I didn't want to go through another divorce, ever. We worked out our respective insecurities over time, taking enough time and learning about one another. We were certainly in love and were engaged after thirteen months of dating and married in less than two years. That sounds like a short time, but we covered all our bases in that time and, other than a few butterflies, were comfortable and excited to take the next step. Now that we've been married for several years, I can honestly say God used the deep pain of my divorce to make me a better person and a better husband. God really is the Lord of second chances. If you're still going through the dark night of the soul, I encourage you to seek His face, ask for forgiveness, and most of all, forgive yourself. The best is yet to come.

You didn't miss it!

9

Rhonda

"For the Lord God is a sun and shield; The Lord will give grace and glory; No good thing will He withhold from those who walk uprightly."

Psalm 84:11

I've always been an "all or nothing" kind of girl. I could go years without dating anyone (not that I liked it much) if I didn't meet someone who interested me. If I liked the guy, he would have known it right away, and I might have come on too strong, potentially scaring him off. Fortunately, with Bill, I didn't realize I liked him as much as I did until much later in our relationship, which gave him a running head-start in his pursuit of me. I was playing "hard to get" without even realizing it! Once again, God was saving me from myself, and I got to enjoy being courted by a gentleman, and Bill got to enjoy the chase.

However, it was nearly Christmas, and I was quite certain "Boyfriend Bill" was going to become "Husband Bill" in short order. Perhaps he would propose at Christmas. My friend Ginna and I sat down at one of our favorite local bistros in Virginia Beach's Town

Center and started planning my "spring wedding." Where should we have it? Who should be invited? Should it be a destination wedding or something quaint and closer to home? What should my colors be? Should I have bridesmaids or just flower girls? It was a deliciously dangerous game I was playing, but I was like a moth to a flame, and I literally could not stop myself from going there.

In full disclosure, I had already tried on a few wedding dresses back in October when my best friend Rhonda, who is from the New Orleans area, came to visit me. Rhonda, who is a lover of "love," could not resist taking me wedding dress shopping before she had to catch her flight back home to Louisiana. I, of course, was more than willing to oblige. Amazingly, we found a bridal boutique that would let me try on dresses without an appointment, a testament to Rhonda's sweet southern charm.

Meanwhile, Bill was duck hunting thousands of miles away in Saskatchewan, Canada. So, while Bill was lying in the tall grass dressed in full camo with a gun at his side, waiting to shoot birds out of the sky, little did he know that his girlfriend was in full wedding mode back home, dreaming of the day he would get down on one knee, hopefully not dressed in camo. On second thought, that might be kind of sexy, but once again, I'm getting ahead of myself. And ladies, I know I am not alone in playing this fairytale fantasy game, nor am I alone in feeling the heartbreak that comes when you get out of God's timing, but more about that later.

Although Rhonda and I did not find "the dress" that day, it was still fun to dream, play, and plan for a wedding that, at least for the moment, did not seem that far off. Rhonda had been (and still is) my number one prayer partner since we first met in February of 2014, right after my book *You Are a Prize to Be Won, Don't Settle for Less than God's Best* was released. I was in Nashville for the annual National Religious Broadcasters meeting and bumped into my good friend, Becky Alonzo, along with Rhonda Gray, whom I had yet to meet, at the beautiful Gaylord Opryland Resort & Convention Center. I had interviewed Becky at her Nashville home a few years back about her amazing book and testimony, *The Devil in Pew Number 7*. It's an incredible story of how a jealous neighbor shot her precious father and mother, who pastored a small church in North Carolina. Becky's mother was killed instantly, but her father lived for a few more years but was never the same. I'm blessed to receive a lot of books to read and review at CBN, but I could not put Becky's down. It not only keeps you on the edge of your seat, but it's a testament to God's faithfulness in the midst of the worst pain imaginable. Becky was eventually able to forgive her parents' killer—another part of her amazing testimony.

Meanwhile, I was tired from pulling my little black suitcase stuffed with a couple dozen copies of my new book all over the Gaylord, which is really like a small indoor city. I was hoping to run into someone who would want to help me promote it or, hey, even buy a copy! That was when I saw a familiar face in the gift shop I had stopped to browse in—my beautiful friend Becky. We hugged, and she introduced me to the pretty blonde woman next to her. Rhonda couldn't wait to hear my story (the one in my book about my heartbreak). And even though I had "been there, done that, had the t-shirt, and wrote a book about it"—literally! I was still hurting from the pain of being rejected and feeling betrayed. Rhonda, who is also a pastor, could sense I was growing weary in the waiting and needed some encouragement. She prayed for me right there in the gift shop; we exchanged numbers, and that began the most profound friendship of my lifetime.

For the next three and a half years, Rhonda stood in faith with me by prayer, texts, cards, visits, and lots and lots of phone calls—encouraging me that God was going to bring me not just a husband but His best and the desire of my heart. On the days when I just couldn't wait one more day, I would call my friend in tears, and she would lend me her faith, pray for me, remind me of God's goodness and faithfulness, and give me scriptures to back it up like Psalm 84:11, *"No good thing will He withhold from those who walk uprightly."*

I can't tell you how many times I saw that scripture on a text or a card, along with Ephesians 3:20, *"Now to Him who is able to do exceedingly abundantly above all that we ask or think, according to the power that works in us."* God promises us that His words will not return to Him void, and Rhonda knew that and kept giving me the Word over and over.

I was forty-nine when I met Rhonda, and with each passing day, month, and year, her friendship, faith, and our prayers together became more important. You might say that God sent Rhonda to be my lifeline and keep my faith afloat when doubt, discouragement, or just sheer weariness in the waiting were about to take me under. She often reminded me that God had chosen her to "keep her face to the carpet" on behalf of women like me who were waiting for their future husbands. Rhonda was my spiritual mid-wife, helping me to push through the dark days, the days of doubt, and to believe and know that God was going to do all He had promised and more—simply because I was His daughter and His Word promised that He would give me the desires of my heart if I was putting Him first (Psalm 37:4).

Although Rhonda married at twenty-seven, she could still identify with waiting because she had wanted to be married years earlier but had to taste heartbreak and date a few counterfeits before she met her match. Today, she and her husband, Curtis, pastor a wonderful church in Slidell, Louisiana, called "Grace Fellowship." Curtis and my husband, Bill, are great friends and fishing buddies. But those three and a half years between when my book came out and I met my husband were the "testing" years.

I was now in my early fifties and wondering if God had forgotten me, although I knew in my heart that He had not. I would often pray late at night up in my "prayer loft" on the third floor of my condo. One particular night (I think I was fifty-one at the time) I was on my knees praying the same prayer I had prayed many times before, asking the Lord to bring my husband. That is when I heard the unmistakable voice of the Holy Spirit in my own spirit saying, "When you're ready, there he will be." "But Lord, I am ready!" I politely argued with the Father. I heard nothing back in return but knew that God knows me better than I know myself, and if He said I wasn't quite ready, then I wasn't ready. I reminded God that I had dedicated my book *You Are a Prize to Be Won* to my future husband! "God, please don't let me be ashamed!" I would beg. I had dedicated my book in faith, and I didn't want to lose that faith now—especially when I was so close; at least I prayed I was.

10

Ice-Skating

"I just want my life to be a Hallmark Christmas movie."

—Unknown

Fast-forward back to late December 2017, and I was pretty sure I had the perfect Christmas-time "date-night" idea—ice-skating! After spending most of my single years addicted to Hallmark movies—especially the Christmas ones where there is at least one romantic ice-skating scene per movie—I asked Bill if he'd like to go to the local ice skating rink with me. I could see us now—hand in hand as we flew over the ice in perfect harmony with tiny snowflakes tickling our noses, but apparently that only happens in the movies; the reality was somewhat different.

However, as luck would have it, we had to walk through the shopping mall in downtown Norfolk on our way to the rink, and lo and behold, there was a jewelry store with lots of sparkly diamonds in the window. Naturally, I stopped to admire them. Bill noticed and asked if I'd like to go inside. I landed right in front of the case with all the engagement rings—go figure!

The nice older lady behind the glass case asked if I would like to try something on. "Yes, please!" I said with eager anticipation. "How about that one!" I exclaimed as I admired the sparkly solitaire in the white gold setting surrounded by smaller diamonds now wrapped around my ring finger. I was impressed with how cool and composed Bill looked, as if my trying on engagement rings was the most natural thing in the world. Yes, maybe I was being a bit obvious, but Bill, I could tell, was enjoying the fact that I was looking toward a future with him, and nothing in his demeanor said he was scared.

But that was about to change once we hit the ice. Bill, I discovered, does not like to ice-skate. In fact, I would say he pretty much hated it and held on to the side rails most of the time. The few times he let go, he had a look of terror on his face that still makes me giggle. Interestingly, he's a very good snow skier, but apparently one doesn't make you good at the other. Still, I had a blast as I spun around in circles showing off my best Dorothy Hamill moves.

Later that night, we went back to my condo, sat under my Christmas tree, and exchanged gifts. Bill, I discovered, is a great gift-giver! One of my many "love" languages, and apparently he'd been listening because he got me the most incredible pair of cowboy boots I have ever owned! The kind that look and feel like they've already been worn by a real cowboy for years and came adorned with a very cool western motif that I just loved. The funny thing was he thought my shoe size was eight and a half, but I'm a nine or nine and a half in shoes and sometimes a ten in boots, but these size eight and a half cowboy boots fit perfectly—like they were made for me. If you knew how much trouble I have finding shoes and especially boots that fit, you would certainly think this was a sign from the heavens—I know I did. Bill opened his gift from me: a caramel-colored leather bomber jacket with a collar, the kind of jacket you can dress up or down. It looked great with his dark brown hair. The leather was so soft and included that real leather coat smell that I love. Our first Christmas gifts, but ones that I'm pretty sure will last a lifetime.

Keep in mind, Bill had not even hinted at proposing, but he had told me he loved me—I think. We were standing in line waiting for our order at McDonald's after a full day of hiking in the Blue Ridge Mountains back in August when I heard him say, "I love ya." I was too stunned to say anything at the time, so I waited until we got back in the car and asked him if he had said I love ya—and if that meant the same thing as I love you.

I was flashing back to that scene in the movie *Something's Gotta Give* where Jack Nicholson's character, Harry Sanborn, an aging lady's man says, "I love ya," to Diane Keaton's character, Erica Barry. Barry is a successful playwright in her mid-fifties who was falling fast for the smooth-talking Sanborn. Barry answered, "Well, I love you too! If that's what you said. I don't know if it ends in a 'ya' if it's a true 'I love you.'" To which Sanborn replies, "You're not like anybody."

Bill told me he didn't remember the exact exchange but did recall that we had enjoyed a great day hiking in the mountains, were traveling home, and were starving for some healthy food! "Naturally, McDonald's came into view," Bill recalled. He went on to say, "We were standing in line goofing around, joking, laughing, and probably making some juvenile display. Wendy has a sharp wit, which I am often the target of, and she makes me laugh on a regular basis. She said something profoundly funny in that line, and we were having such a great time, it just came out, 'I love ya.' As a typical male, I didn't think about the details, implications, or the spelling, but I did mean it!" Bill said.

I decided not to tell Bill I loved him back—at least not yet. I thought, *I'm going to savor those words, hide them in my heart for a while, and just enjoy the fact that he said them.* More importantly, I was going to wait until it was a "you"—not a "ya"—just to make sure he understood the significance of those three little words, well, in this case, two and a half words, but if I'd learned anything from my last relationship, it was not to be the first one to say "I love you."

In my last serious relationship, when my then-boyfriend finally said those coveted three little words, he put a "but" after them. He said, "I love you, but I don't know if you're the one." I recall, in my book *You Are a Prize to Be Won*, it was like getting kissed and slapped at the same time. I had wanted to hear those words so badly, but when I finally did, it felt more like I'd just been punched in the gut. I remember feeling a bit sick to my stomach afterward, and it was so confusing to me because, at that time, I didn't know that I deserved much more than an "I love you, but"—I deserved an I love you period, but despite God telling me years earlier that I was a "prize to be won," I still didn't know it. If you're dating someone with the goal of marriage and they say, "I love you, but..." please know they are keeping their options open and they're not really sure they love you at all. If I could do that moment over, I would have kindly told him to take his "but" and his "butt" back to where he came from because I was worthy of an I love you—period—and so are you. Never settle for an I love you "but." Having learned that lesson the hard way, I was more than willing to ponder Bill's "I love ya!" in my heart until his "ya" became a "you" and I was certain that I felt the same way.

11

The Blizzard of 2018

"Do not rush. Trust. And keep a quiet heart."

—Elizabeth Elliot

It was just a few days after Bill and I rang in our first New Year's together, and everyone was focused on taking down their Christmas lights and getting back to work when the blizzard of 2018 slapped the East Coast, including the Hampton Roads area, with one of the biggest snowstorms on record. Winds topped more than forty miles per hour as more than ten inches of snow turned my neighborhood in Chesapeake into a shimmering snow globe. One meteorologist called it "an absolute coastal bomb," and for the Norfolk area, it ranked twelfth for all-time record snowfall events. And it wasn't just us— almost the entire East Coast was covered in snow. The historic storm, also dubbed a "snow bomb cyclone"—basically, a winter hurricane— dumped over a foot of snow in New England but also brought with it damaging winds and dangerous, icy coastal flooding. But here in Chesapeake, we mainly got the beauty without the danger.

I love snow, so this was a dream come true for me, as our area rarely sees this kind of snowfall. The evening before, Bill had stopped by for dinner after spending the afternoon deer hunting on the Eastern Shore of Virginia. Deer season was nearly over, and Bill had harvested a nice-size doe, which was now in a cooler in the bed of his pick-up. The unseasonably cold weather was sufficient to keep the venison nice and cold. When the snow began to fall late Wednesday, we decided it was best for him to stay in my guestroom. He lived a thirty-minute drive away, and I didn't want to take a chance on him sliding off the road. On January 4th, we awoke to a winter wonderland. The snowdrifts were over a foot high in some places, and a beautiful sparkly white blanket covered the ground. It was picture-perfect. Bill's doe was now frozen in the cooler and covered with snow...at least he wouldn't have to worry about the meat spoiling. Bill, true to form, was up early and out in the parking lot helping my neighbors shovel their cars out of the high snow drifts. Dressed in his camo coat, blue jeans tucked into his snow boots, and a maroon Virginia Tech toboggan, Bill worked tirelessly to erase the blizzard's bounty while, at the same time, laughing and talking with a few of my neighbors.

Although we'd been dating for six months, I felt like I was seeing Bill with fresh eyes, or rather God was showing me his character in a way that I hadn't seen or realized (at least not to this extent) before. And what I was seeing was not only heart-warming but sexy! Here he was, out shoveling snow, laughing with my neighbors, taking charge, and helping others. It was very attractive, and although Bill is handsome, he became even more handsome to me after this.

Later that morning, bundled up from head to toe, Bill and I ventured out for a nice long walk in what still looked like a winter wonderland. Bill playfully grabbed a huge icicle off a building, about the size of his arm, and held it like a sword as I snapped several pictures. I can't remember what we talked about, but I do remember how peaceful and perfect that day seemed. Bill, who is a vice president at a local financial institution, did not have to go to work that day, and neither did I. The blizzard of 2018 had shut everything down. The only thing open that evening was the 7-Eleven. Thank heaven for 7-Eleven!

The next day, everything was still shut down, so Bill and I volunteered to shovel snow with Operation Blessing, the Christian Broadcasting Network's humanitarian outreach organization. Turns out there were a lot of elderly people or handicapped people who needed assistance with snow removal. They simply weren't able to shovel that much snow from their walkways or driveways. And although most people were happy to be hunkered down inside next to a cozy fire, some felt safer knowing that, if necessary, they could at least get their cars out of the garage and down the driveway without difficulty. Operation Blessing sent us out with some other like-minded folks for an afternoon of "Operation Snow Removal."

Snow, it turns out, gets pretty heavy after you've shoveled enough of it. Our arms and backs were sore, but all in all, it was a fun day helping others with a few snowball fights thrown in. Once again, God was showing me Bill's character, his work ethic, his love for the outdoors—his fun nature. Although the snow had stopped falling, I was falling more in love during the blizzard of 2018; that was for sure.

Take a Snow Day

When it snows, everything gets quiet—businesses shut down, school children rejoice when they hear they're getting a "snow day," and even countries at war have paused fighting because of snow. It's as if the heavens are saying, "Not today—take a day off. Stop everything—enjoy a 'snow day.'"

It was also a prophetic picture of what 2018 would be like for me. I was in a hurry, but God wasn't. I was fifty-three years old and, with each passing day, getting more restless and tired of waiting to be a bride and for my prince charming to get down on one knee and ask me to marry him already!

My journal entries from early 2018 are filled with scriptures about waiting:

On 1/25/18 I heard God say, "If you wait, you will be blessed." *"For they shall not be ashamed who wait for Me"* (Isaiah 49:23).

On 1/26 my friend Ginna sent me a text, "Just wait until you see why God had you wait. What God is doing is beyond what you could even pray or think of."

On 1/28, at the top of the page, I wrote the word "wait" and the scripture, *"Therefore, the Lord will wait, that He may be gracious to you. And therefore, He will be exalted, that He may have mercy on you. For the Lord is a God of Justice. Blessed are all those who wait for Him"* (Isaiah 30:18).

Waiting = grace, mercy, blessings, and God will be exalted.

In early April, for some unknown reason, the waiting had turned into an almost tangible heaviness—I prayed and asked the Lord what to do, and again I heard, "Wait." I prayed, "Lord, show me how to wait well and glorify You in the waiting."

Even in July, I wrote in my journal, "I keep getting scriptures on waiting" and wrote the following scriptures down as a reminder:

"Wait on the Lord; Be of good courage, And He shall strengthen your heart; Wait, I say, on the Lord!" (Psalm 27:14).

"Therefore, I will look to the Lord; I will wait for the God of my salvation, My God will hear me" (Micah 7:7).

I even wrote the definition down, "Wait: To tarry, hope, trust, expect, be patient, remain in anticipation."

On July 11th, I read the following in my beloved devotional *Streams in the Desert* by L. B. Cowman:

> *"God will often extricate us from the mess we have made, because 'his love endures forever.'" (1 Chron. 16:34) Yet, if we had only been patient and waited to see the unfolding of His plan, we would never have found ourselves in such an impossible maze, seeing no way out. We would also never have had to turn back and retrace our way, with wasted steps and so many tears of shame.*

"Wait for the Lord" (Psalm 27:14).
"Patiently Wait!"

—F. B. Meyer

God was asking me to be patient. Maybe right now, He's asking you to be patient as well. Patient with God, patient with yourself, and patient with your circumstances. You see, God was at work. God was working on me, and He was working on Bill. And right now, if you're reading this and still waiting, be encouraged. God is at work in you too. Be patient, take a "snow day," and trust God's timing.

You didn't miss it!

12

The Proposal

"Blessed is she who believed, for there will be a fulfillment of those things which were told her from the Lord."

Luke 1:45

September 1, 2018, was a Saturday, and I was looking forward to climbing my favorite mountain in Virginia—Old Rag. I'd lost count of how many times I had trekked up her rugged peaks—nearly a hundred times for sure, but the majestic views of the Blue Ridge Mountains and the challenge of summitting one of the most difficult hikes in the Shenandoah National Forest, kept me coming back for more. This time, I was with my boyfriend, Bill, and our friend Ginna, the one who had introduced us the summer before. It was hot and muggy, and we were sweating like crazy but having a great time as we talked and laughed our way to the top. I was glad to be getting this hike in because, in one week, Ginna and I were leaving for Chamonix, France, for the *Tour de Mont Blanc*, a six-day hiking trek through the breath-taking hills and valleys of the French, Italian, and Swiss Alps. I was in pretty good shape, but I knew I'd feel better and more confident about "the tour" if I got in one more hike up Old Rag, which usually takes me about five and a half hours round-trip.

As we approached the summit, somehow the topic of marriage popped up. Ginna had gone on ahead of us, and it was just Bill and me. As we navigated around this large granite rock, I remember playfully saying how singleness had its advantages but then jokingly added, "But I might consider marrying you." He just smiled and said something similar back. The flirting was fun, and Bill and I were in a good place. After quickly getting over not getting a ring back in the summer, when I thought it might happen, I was now enjoying the ride and letting God and Bill lead. Plus, I had a big adventure coming up and another mountain—or in this case mountains—to climb. Life was good.

Finally, we made it to the top—3,284 feet if you're wondering—not the highest mountain in Virginia but certainly one of the most challenging and fun to hike. However, I was shocked to see the summit completely enveloped in a thick, dense fog. Normally, you could see ridge after ridge of the breathtaking Blue Ridge Mountains, brilliant blue skies, and sometimes an eagle circling above. This time, however, you could barely see the rock right in front of you. This was very unusual, and I was so disappointed, as this was Ginna's first time on Old Rag and I really wanted her to experience the full beauty of this special mountain, especially the amazing views at the top!

Will You Carry This Down the Mountain?

Bill and I had hiked Old Rag the previous summer, so he knew how incredible it was. Nevertheless, it was lunchtime, and we sat down on my favorite rock, took our sandwiches and apples out of our backpacks, and enjoyed the fact that we had made it to the summit. Then, to make matters more interesting, it started to thunder and lightning, and there was a light drizzle of rain. As we were taking the last bites of our sandwiches, I mentioned that we'd better get going and was about to stand up when Bill asked me to wait a minute because he wasn't quite ready. A few seconds later, I looked over at Bill, and he was looking at me and holding a diamond ring in his hand—he simply said, "Will you carry this down the mountain?" I was like a deer in headlights—my eyes kept bouncing from the ring (which was spectacular) to Bill's face and back to the ring, and after watching way too many Hallmark romance movies, I just knew there had to be more words coming from Bill, so I just kept starring at him for what seemed like an eternity. Finally, I couldn't take it any longer and said, "Is there something you want to ask me?" Clearly, the ring said it all—but Bill took the hint and said, "Will you marry me?"

Sitting on top of my favorite mountain, covered with sweat and rain, I said yes as Bill slipped the most beautiful engagement ring—a 2 kt. solitaire with tiny diamonds wrapped around the white gold band onto my finger. Oh, how I had dreamed of this day—but in my dreams, I was in the quintessential little black dress at an elegant restaurant surrounded by soft light and music, and my make-up was, at least, on, but this was way better! It was perfect. Ginna had missed the whole thing because a few minutes earlier, she'd gotten spooked by the thunder and moved behind the rock we were on. Looking back, I'm glad we had that moment to ourselves. Then, as if on cue, she reappeared just seconds after Bill proposed. Speechless, all I could do was hold out my hand for her to see!

Bill had not told anyone, including Ginna, of his plans, so she was just as shocked as I was. We took dozens of photos and celebrated the moment as best as we could before more thunder and lightning forced us to start our descent. I practically floated down the mountain as I kept gazing at the stunning sparkler now on my left hand. The fact that it was gray and overcast made the ring dazzle all the more brightly! I was truly surprised! I know a lot of women know it's coming, but getting engaged on this day was the farthest thing from my mind, although I had certainly hoped it would happen sooner rather than later. The conversation during our two-and-a-half-hour trip down the mountain was mainly about the ring. I found out that day *why* we didn't get engaged back in the summer—the ring wasn't ready! Bill had searched for six months and done his homework and did not want to settle for a lesser diamond. I was happy he waited.

Like a Scene Right Out of a Movie

What I didn't realize at the time was I had written this very proposal scene in a movie script I had finished about a month before I met Bill. The screenplay was based loosely on my book *You Are a Prize to Be Won* and was called *I Love You But...* A romantic comedy based on the very single Sydney—a.k.a. me—and a guy named Ben who would become Sydney's fiancé in the movie.

It's important to note here that Bill had never read my book (I wouldn't let him since it was about another guy), and he didn't know I had written a screenplay about it. I had finished it before I met Bill, and it was just sitting on the shelf—where it still remains—but I believe the Lord wanted me to write it, so, hopefully, one day, it will be on the big screen or little screen (Netflix).

Amazingly and prophetically, I had written the proposal scene, which took place on the very rock we were sitting on at the top of my beloved Old Rag. Here is that scene from my screenplay *I Love You But...*

(Autumn—leaves falling)

Ext. Old Rag Mountain—Ben and Sydney reach the summit of Old Rag

Ben: I'm so glad you could meet me here—I wanted to get one last good hike in before the weather turned.

Sydney: Remember the last time we were here, and you tried to sit on my rock?

Ben: You mean my rock...

Sydney: Well, okay. How about we make it "*our*" rock?

Ben: I like that. And speaking of rocks... (Ben pulls a ring box out of his backpack)

Sydney: Oh my Gosh! Ben, what...

Ben: Sydney, You're the woman I've always dreamed of. You're beautiful, smart, adventurous; you make me laugh...you make me crazy, and you make me a better man...will you marry me?

Sydney: Of course I will.

(Kiss)

Bill finally understood why I was expecting "more words." I had written this very moment before I met him. When I showed him this scene, he was amazed but not that surprised. "You love this place so much, there couldn't be any other spot to propose to you." He also added, "Ben's words for you at the end are accurate for you, too, my dear!"

Hibiscus Hope

When we got back to Virginia Beach, I noticed my favorite hibiscus flower plant outside my front door had a beautiful red bloom on it. After flowering all summer long, it had just suddenly stopped, and I couldn't remember the last time there was a bloom. But today, as if celebrating my proposal, there it was, smiling back at me. I took a photo of my hand with my new ring with the flower in the background. Then, strangely, as I went to take the trash to the dumpster, I saw a car with a vanity plate that read "hibiscus." See, this is how God gets my attention. Clearly, He wanted to speak to me through the hibiscus flower, so I promptly looked up the meaning, and to my wonder this is what it said:

"The hibiscus flower, the official state flower of Hawaii, is considered very feminine. Red hibiscus flowers symbolize passion and deep romantic love. In North America especially, hibiscus flowers are used to symbolize the perfect woman or wife" (Florgeous.com).

Clearly, I was under no grand illusions that I would be able to pull off perfection as a wife, but I knew God was using this simple flower—my favorite tropical flower in all the world—to give me hope that I could, at the very least, be a good wife and that God would help me to be the best wife I could be to my husband.

"I'm Writing Your Story"

The day after the proposal, Bill and I were attending services at New Life Church in Virginia Beach. As the worship music played and everyone was singing, I spoke to God about the fog on the mountain the day before, "Lord, I just don't understand why on such a perfect day—the day of my proposal—the entire mountain was fogged in." I instantly heard His voice reply, "I'm writing your story." In other words, as much as I wanted to see into the future and know what God's plans were, I was going to have to trust God every step of the way. He wasn't going to give it all away! Psalm 119:105 says, "*You word is a lamp to my feet and a light to my path.*" He doesn't show us everything; He only shows us the next step, but He lights our way—even through the thickest fog. I would trust Him.

13

Leap of Faith

"Now faith is the substance of things hoped for,
the evidence of those things not seen."

Hebrews 11:1

Exactly one week after Bill proposed to me, Ginna and I arrived in Chamonix, France, a charming French village at the base of the famous Mount Blanc, the highest summit in the Alps, to prepare for our next hiking adventure—the *Tour du Mont Blanc*. The TMB is one of the most popular long-distance treks in Europe that takes you on a circuit through the magnificent French, Italian, and Swiss Alps and covers about 110 miles. We would do an eight-day, fifty-mile version of the tour, averaging about seven hours of hiking each day. Although breathtakingly beautiful, the trek is very challenging, with extreme inclines and descents along the way. Thankfully, the elevation is not that high—between 3,200 and 8,800 feet at its highest, making for a more enjoyable journey without the worry of altitude sickness. In the evenings, we were rewarded with delicious dinners and hot showers at the various picturesque inns along the way.

Ginna was co-leading this trek with our French mountain guide, Bruno, a seasoned mountaineer with more than thirty years of hiking experience in the Alps. He knew "the Tour" like the back of his hand and, despite being in his late fifties, was the fastest guy in the group and always smiling like this was his first time doing the TMB.

Although this trip had been planned for months and was on my list of must-do hikes, I never dreamed I'd be going as a newly engaged woman! The feeling was a bit surreal. I was thankful for this time to process the fact that I was now engaged to be married! Again, the reality of those words had not yet sunk in. A few days prior on *The 700 Club*, I proudly showed off my beautiful diamond solitaire engagement ring to a worldwide audience. While still on the air, CBN founder and *700* co-host, Pat Robertson, looked at me and exclaimed, "You're getting married!" The realization of those words hit me for the very first time—this wasn't just a fantasy! This absolutely dazzling ring on my finger was a promise of a lifetime together with another person! It was the thing I'd been asking God for and praying for and writing about and journaling about for what seemed like forever! So why did I suddenly feel, um, that I needed more time? Believe it or not, even though I was just one week shy of my fifty-fourth birthday, I was glad I would have a week hiking through the Alps to let the reality of this moment and the significance of this ring on my left hand sink in.

Leap of Faith

The weather for our trek could not have been better. It was unseasonably warm and sunny for our journey—shorts and T-shirts and a light jacket did the job, as each day was more beautiful than the next. To be honest, I only knew we had left France and had crossed over into Italy because suddenly, instead of *bonjour*, fellow hikers on the trail were saying, "*Ciao!*" (which means hello and goodbye in Italian). Large herds of white sheep and black cows dotted the lush green hills as we climbed up, down, and around what can only be described as a picture postcard.

Although there were plenty of fellow hikers to walk and talk with, it was also the perfect time for thinking, praying, and processing all that had just happened and was about to happen in my life. I know this is going to sound crazy, but looking back, I believe God gave me this week to not only celebrate being newly engaged but also to say goodbye to my single life—the only life I had ever known, and perhaps because I was an older single, I really needed this time to reflect and ponder my future.

As I prayed, one thing I was beginning to realize was—no matter what, marriage would be a step of faith.

Bill and I had only known each other for thirteen months. We had been through all the holidays together, including our birthdays—and did I mention he got me the most exquisite cowboy boots for our first Christmas together that actually fit even though they were the wrong size! After that, I just knew that he was "the one." And there were many more signs, but were those signs enough to say "I do" for the rest of my life?

Of course, you want to be in love, equally yoked, and feel that you're going in the same or at least a compatible direction with your spouse with God as your pilot. But I also felt that God was showing me that I would still need to take a step of faith, a step into the unknown. I knew that I felt peace and that my family and friends really liked Bill. Looking back, those were two things that were missing in my last relationship. There was no peace, and I found out later—my family did not care for him. Listen to your friends and family. They can often see and sense things you can't.

This time, though, there was peace but also a sense of not just taking a step of faith—but rather a leap of faith off a high cliff. Don't get me wrong; it felt exciting but a little scary at the same time. And I don't care how in love you are, marriage *is* a leap of faith, and one not only worth taking with the right person but one that I believe God delights in, for the Bible says, "*Without faith it is impossible to please Him*" (Hebrews 11:6). I was now ready to take the leap for love.

14

The Wedding of the Century

"I have found the one my soul loves."

Song of Solomon 3:4

It was the wedding of the century. No, I'm not referring to the royal wedding of Princess Kate and Prince William, although admittedly, that was spectacular, and I watched every second of it on television. I'm referring to the wedding of Wendy and William—just commoners, but on this day, they were royalty, the prince and princess of their own regal wedding set not at Windsor Castle but a castle nonetheless: the beautiful and iconic Homestead Resort, nestled in the foothills of southern Virginia's majestic Blue Ridge Mountains.

Flashback: Summer 2011

I thought I might be falling in love with the guy I was dating. I hadn't really even liked him that much at the beginning, but then, suddenly, without warning, I thought he could be the one. The fact that I was forty-six going on forty-seven at the end of the summer was possibly one of the reasons. At any rate, I was driving west on I-64 on my way to visit my parents in West Virginia when I saw the exit sign for the Homestead, a place of some of my favorite childhood memories. It was the '70s. I was ten years old, and my two sisters were nine and five the first time we visited this magical place that at the time felt like a palace. My two younger brothers were not even born yet (they missed the '70s for the most part), but I'll never forget the fun we had ice-skating at the top of the mountain and how my parents, aunts, and uncles dressed up for dinner. Back then, it was mandatory black tie, and my mom and my aunt Jeanie looked like princesses, and my dad, who has always been handsome and still is, looked like a movie star in his black tie and tux. My mom wore this glamorous black dress with gold flecks and rhinestones at the top and black feathers at the bottom that is still, to this day, one of the most beautiful evening gowns I've ever seen. Sadly, they just don't make dresses like that anymore. I have it in my closet now—and was last able to get it zipped about twenty years ago, but I still have hope. Our family visited the Homestead for several years during the '70s, mostly at Thanksgiving or Christmas, so suffice it to say, it was a place close to my heart.

On a whim, I decided to pull off the highway and drive the sixteen miles of curvy mountainous road to visit the Homestead. It had been years since I'd been there, and I was curious if it still looked and "felt" the same. Finally, I arrived. Funny how things aren't as big when you get older, and of course, by now, I had traveled the world and had been in literal castles, but still, something about this place felt like home. I couldn't help but think that this would be a great place to get married—maybe soon! So I asked to see their wedding brochure. Wow! I had no idea weddings were this expensive. Hmmm...maybe it won't be here...after a visit to the resort's gift shop, it was time to leave. As I was pulling out, I saw a little green church on the hill next to the Homestead. It was a Presbyterian church, but the denomination didn't matter. I had been to Presbyterian, Baptist, and in recent years preferred mostly non-denominational churches. I decided to check it out and maybe say a prayer. The big wooden doors opened with ease, and I walked inside with no problem. With just me and the sun's rays shining through the stained-glass windows, I got down on my knees in front of the altar and said a simple prayer, "Lord, I'd like to get married at the Homestead someday." Then, I drove to West Virginia and forgot about that prayer for many years.

Rush to the Altar

When Bill proposed to me at the top of Old Rag Mountain on September 1, 2018, it was one of the happiest days of my life! I have to give him credit, though; he really surprised me! I was still in shock, as I just wasn't expecting it at that time for some reason. Anyway, I didn't want to be engaged for long—I was turning fifty-four in two weeks, and well, I'd waited long enough. I went into full-throttle wedding-planning mode. At first, we thought the best scenario would be a destination wedding. I spent hours on the phone with a lovely Jamaican woman only to discover that New Year's was their most expensive season, and the only rooms left were over $1,000 a night. I didn't think my family would have appreciated that, so Jamaica was out. We thought about Virginia Beach, but it just didn't feel right. Then I remembered the Homestead.

I had been there the previous summer for a work retreat and really enjoyed it. Bill and I had only been dating a couple of months then, and we had talked on the phone while I was there, and I sent him a few photos of the beautiful grounds. It had changed so much since I was a kid, new restaurants and shops, and they moved the ice-skating rink to the main grounds, but it still held a timeless and special beauty, and of course, the mountains hadn't changed—they were as majestic as ever.

I remembered the price tag from years ago but decided to check it out again anyway. To my amazement, it was actually doable now, with two of us paying, plus a little help from the bank—this could happen! I had passed the age of relying on my parents to foot the bill and really just wanted them to be there and enjoy themselves. They had raised five kids and paid for more piano lessons, cheerleading uniforms, and tennis shoes than I'm sure they could remember—they deserved a break. Then, I remembered the prayer I had prayed at the little green church years ago, and suddenly, it was a no-brainer. We would get married at the Homestead. Bill loved the idea too. Bill grew up on the water, but he loved the mountains equally from all of his years of deer hunting in the woods, some of it very close to the Homestead.

The Wedding Planner

Esme, a seasoned wedding planner at the Homestead, became my best friend for the next several months. We talked often as we discussed ballrooms, flowers, chairs, food, music, and other details. When I wasn't talking to Esme, I was doodling on napkins, drawing tables, and imagining where all my guests would sit. Wedding planning, I soon discovered, is not only a full-time job; it's an obsession.

With just under a hundred people invited, it would be intimate but not too small to feel festive. And with a smaller group, it would be the most important people in my and Bill's life. We wanted to be surrounded by our family and our true friends. Bill is an only child but was blessed to grow up in the same place we live now and has childhood friends he considers brothers. I moved around a lot as a kid and later as an adult pursuing my broadcasting career but have the advantage of being the oldest of five children, with lots of nieces and nephews—so we have a built-in party wherever we go.

It's My Turn

I couldn't help but think, *It's finally my turn. This is happening, and it's happening to me this time!* My sisters, Jean Anne and Nancy, have always been my best friends and biggest supporters, and they were almost as excited as I was. I had been a bridesmaid in their weddings years ago but decided not to put them through that and just keep it simple. Plus, when you're getting married for the first time at fifty-four, you've earned the right to keep the focus on yourself! My nieces, ten-year-old Kelly Anne and five-year-old Keaton, would be the flower girls. As "head" flower girl, Kelly Anne would keep the younger Keaton on track and make sure she fulfilled her all-important petal-distributing duties, and three of my nephews, eight-year-old

Crew, seven-year-old Alex, and five-year-old Jack, would be the ring bearers. They all wanted to take part, so I couldn't say no. Plus, seeing them in their little tuxes would be priceless.

The Rehearsal Dinner—February 8, 2019

I wore a long sequined red dress with straps that crisscrossed in the back and a little train for extra glam. This was my wedding, and I was going to be the star of the show. My friend Rhonda also wore a long red dress. I had told everyone it was going to be a "black tie" formal weekend and to come prepared—they did! About thirty of us dined on Allegheny Mountain Trout Almandine in the Homestead's main dining room. A full band was entertaining us on the stage near the dance floor and played our wedding theme song, "Moondance," without us even telling them. When I sent out our wedding "e-vites," the only millennial thing I've ever done, I put the song "Moondance" with it—the Michael Bublé version. Van Morrison is the original singer, and he is one of the greats, but for some reason I really liked Bublé's version. At any rate, the band broke into "Moondance," and Bill and I made our way to the dance floor. Dancing on the wooden floor under the sparkling chandeliers in my red sequined dress in the same room my parents would have danced in decades before was magical. It was tempting to dance the night away, but I had to remind myself that a bride needs her beauty sleep. Fortunately our wedding was planned for late afternoon, so I would be able to sleep in.

The Wedding Day

After coffee and one of the Homestead's famous homemade cinnamon donuts (too late to diet now), I retreated back to my luxurious bridal suite with its high ceilings, crown molding, and royal bedding. The wedding wasn't until 5:30 p.m., and I had an appointment to get my hair done around 12:30 p.m., but that wasn't going to happen. Although I didn't feel nervous outwardly, I guess my internal nervous system didn't agree, and I felt like I was going to get a cold sore on my lip! This is not happening today of all days! I held ice on my lip for most of the day and never left the room. Rhonda and Stacy were my only visitors during the day, and I was so thankful they stopped by so we could pray. And what a powerful prayer it was. The Holy Spirit really showed up. There were lots of happy tears and hugs from two of my best friends who had stood with me through singlehood and helped me pray in this day. After they left, it was time to get ready. By the time I got out of the shower, I felt better. There was a knock at the door; it was some beautiful pink roses and a note from Bill.

"I can't wait to marry you. Love, Bill." I cried. This day was really happening. After doing my own hair and make-up (I've had a lot of practice after decades in television), my good friend and CBN wardrobe director, Sherry Wade, arrived to help me get into my wedding dress. She'd been dressing me for years at CBN, and it just felt right for her to be there on this day. Plus, most wedding dresses are not that easy to get into, including mine.

It was time to leave the room. Sherry and Ginna, who had also stopped by to check on me, held my long lace train as we made our way to the elevator and then down the long corridor that was lined with the resort's many shops. I felt excited and could not stop smiling. Several hotel guests stopped and stared as we walked and giggled on our way to the ballroom. Then, while still on our way to the ballroom, I suddenly saw Bill—about sixty feet away. He was walking very quickly, but then he glanced down the hallway, and we saw each other! He jokingly put his hand up to his face like he hadn't seen me and kept going. We both laughed so hard. Tonight was going to be fun.

The Missing Bouquet

After walking through the Thomas Jefferson Parlor, my dad and I carefully walked down the stairs to the beautiful Crystal Ballroom. The guests were seated, and Bill was standing next to Pastor Curtis, Rhonda's husband and our good friend who would marry us. Suddenly, all eyes turned around toward me. I felt a joy so deep, it's hard to explain. People were genuinely happy for me. It's like when you're routing for the underdog or, in this case, the girl who never gave up and believed that good things would happen even "late in the game," so to speak. Their smiles said everything. I made a mental note to try to take it all in and remember every moment that I could. My dad was quiet; I think he was more nervous than I was. The piano player had begun playing a beautiful song we had chosen, and it was time for me to start walking toward the altar when Esme realized that I was not holding my bouquet!

With every eye staring at me and after an uncomfortable silence, I simply announced, "I'm waiting for my bouquet!" Everyone burst out laughing. Finally, my beautiful bouquet of red and white roses arrived, and my Dad, a young-looking eighty-year-old, walked me down the aisle, kissed me on the cheek, and placed my hand in my soon-to-be husband's hand.

Pastor Curtis said a few profound things about love and then invited CBN founder Pat Robertson up to say a blessing over us. Pat and I had become good friends over the many years that I was fortunate to co-host *The 700 Club* with him, and his presence, as well as his beautiful prayer over Bill and me, was very special to us.

Bill and I then walked to a table where we lit the unity candle, then back to the altar, where we said our vows and exchanged rings. "I now pronounce you husband and wife. You may kiss the bride," Pastor Curtis proclaimed. Pat Robertson later told me he'd never seen such a passionate kiss at a wedding. I thought it was "wedding appropriate," but apparently our love was evident for all to see.

Smiling from ear to ear, Bill and I left the altar hand in hand and made our way quickly to the back of the room, where our photographer was waiting to whisk us outside and up the hill for the iconic wedding photo with the Homestead at sunset behind us. It was February in the mountains, but I didn't feel the cold at all. Although I wanted some beautiful wedding pictures, I couldn't help thinking about all the fun my guests were having back in the Jefferson Parlor, and I couldn't wait to join them for the reception. After a few pics outside and dozens inside with my family and Bill's parents, it was finally time to join the party!

Bill's Thoughts on the Wedding

The Crystal Ballroom was transformed from a beautiful wedding venue to a reception hall fit for a king and queen. The DJ introduced us and played our wedding theme song, "It's a marvelous night for a moondance..." Bill led me by the hand onto the dance floor and twirled me around as our guests watched and smiled. Afterward, we moved to the head table, where we had a perfect view of our friends and family. Will and Ginna were among the special guests seated there because without them (and Jesus) none of this would be happening. My brother Truman, who is a trial lawyer and the funniest one in the family, made a hilarious speech about Bill that I'm pretty sure he was making up as he went along, and my sister Jean Anne and my cousin Lizzy gave beautiful and heartfelt speeches that nearly made me cry. I made another mental note to embrace every spectacular moment because this was a marvelous night to remember.

The DJ played all of our favorite songs (many of them from the 1980s) and a few country tunes that Bill and I liked for slow dancing. I chose Chaka Khan's "This Time" for our "first dance." I had always loved this song, but it didn't translate that well on the dance floor for some reason. However, if you get a chance, check out the lyrics; it's beautiful. I literally danced the night away, maybe sitting for a couple of songs, but for the most part, I was dancing.

At one point later in the evening, I remember dancing with my beautiful nieces and nephews; there were so many young people on the dance floor, and they added a lot of fun to the party. Also, my parents, who've always been amazing dancers, shared a special song to mark their wedding anniversary, which had been the day before. As the clock ticked toward 11 p.m. and the crowd thinned a bit, yours truly was still on the dance floor. The DJ announced the last song, and with that, I grabbed Bill, and we rocked out to AC/DC's "You Shook Me All Night Long."

Afterward, we headed to one of the resort's beautiful restaurants that didn't close until 1 a.m., where we talked and laughed with those who weren't quite ready to call it a night. Finally, it was me, Bill, Pastor Curtis and Rhonda, and a few others. We were the last ones standing. How fitting because Rhonda had stood by me for so many years while I waited for this night to come, and it finally did. I didn't want this night to end.

If you're wondering how the wedding night went, I'll just say this:

There was such a wonderful feeling of peace. That cloud of shame that I felt when I was younger and looking for love in all the wrong places just wasn't there! No more thinking *I shouldn't have done that* and wondering if he'd call the next day.

Instead, there was a tangible peace, a feeling that God was smiling on this and that it was good. God promises to bless the marriage bed, and He does (Hebrews 13:4)! God is so faithful. If you are tired of feeling the shame that goes with sex before marriage, I encourage you to wait until you're in the loving covenant of marriage. God isn't holding out on you—He's trying to protect your heart. I promise it's worth the wait. You didn't miss it.

My fourth day climbing Mt. Kilimanjaro and we can
finally see the snow-capped summit! Still, the hardest
physical challenge I've ever done.

The first time I met Bill. June 25, 2017 with Ginna and Will
at the Hilton Hotel, Virginia Beach Oceanfront

Ginna and I in Cusco, Peru getting ready to hike the Inca Trial to Machu Picchu!

Newly engaged atop a fogged in Old Rag
Mountain in the Shenandoah National Forest
of Virginia. September 1, 2018.

I never wanted this night to end. Dancing with my
new husband in the Homestead's Crystal Ballroom,
February 9, 2019.

Our African Safari Honeymoon in Tanzania was magical.
I can't wait to go back. February 2019

Date night at one of our favorite restaurants on the water.
Virginia Beach, August 2017.

Right after we said, "I do." The smiles say it all.

The last day of our African honeymoon when we jumped out of the van to take a photo with Mt. Kilimanjaro in the background. Our driver's name was "God Listened" and He surely did.

Rhonda and I enjoying a latte at Cafe' Moka in Virginia Beach. Rhonda prayed with me consistently for years and never stopped encouraging me that God would do all He promised! She was right. Psalm 84:11

Our dear friends Pastors Curtis & Rhonda Gray visiting us in Virginia Beach the same year Pastor Curtis married us. So much to celebrate. October 2019.

Ben and Cheri Martin on their wedding day, Nov. 3, 2012 on Pensacola Beach. Their incredible love story gave me hope when I was still single and I know it will do the same for you. Chapter 22

One of the many reasons I fell in love with Bill. I can't resist a man who hunts and fishes and wears camo. (It's the country girl in me, Bill says I just want the food! Also true) Bill duck hunting in Saskatchewan, Canada, October 2017.

After a whirlwind romance, Stacy & Nick wed in a simple backyard bbq wedding on June 11, 2017, Springfield, Missouri. See Chapter 21 for their incredible love story.

Jemimah and Alister's wedding day. Cape Town, South Africa, October 2021. Their amazing love story is in Chapter 20.

15

Africa

"It was wildest, untouched Africa, and it was magic."

—Jane Goodall

Africa has a way of getting into your soul like no other place I have visited on the earth. Like Jane Goodall aptly said, there's a wildness and a mystery to Africa that can't be explained well in words. When I was there in 2014 climbing the continent's highest peak, Mount Kilimanjaro, the seeds were already being planted for my next visit. After the grueling six-day trek to the summit, I rewarded myself by going on my first safari in Tanzania with several of my fellow hikers who I had met just a week before. I was turning fifty in a week and wanted to do something epic for this epic birthday! What I didn't know before I arrived was how incredibly majestic and romantic watching lions, cheetahs, elephants, and giraffes roam on the Serengeti would be. Well, the potential for romance was there, not so much with a group of near strangers, but I made a mental note that this would be a fabulous honeymoon destination—and it was.

February 14, 2019—Tanzania

From the moment Bill and I arrived at Kilimanjaro International Airport in Arusha, Tanzania, the adventure began. Our driver for the week, Fredy, a young, handsome, and energetic Tanzanian, picked us up in his olive-green safari Jeep and took us directly to a picnic lunch, which was conveniently located near some great souvenir shopping. Although a little travel weary, we enjoyed being pampered as Fredy presented a variety of delicacies for us to try. Then, we loaded up on a collection of African handcrafts, including an exquisitely carved elephant, wooden bowls with delicate etchings of giraffes and zebras, and a faux lion tooth necklace just for fun.

It was Valentine's Day, and after a couple of hours driving through the rugged countryside, we arrived at our oasis, The Lake Manyara Treehouse Lodge. A group of about fifteen or so staff, from the maître d' to the chef, greeted us at the dirt road entrance with a song, some cool drinks, and warm African smiles. After so many lonely Valentine's Days, this was going to be a Valentine's Day and night to remember.

Our treehouse, nestled in the jungle, was even more magical than the pictures I'd seen online, and it could not have been more romantic—from the canopied bed with the mesh mosquito netting to the drawn bath sprinkled with red flower petals to the monkeys playing with the outdoor shower head out on the deck, this was paradise. But it was not without danger, as lions, leopards, and elephants roamed at night, so after dark, we had to be escorted back to our treehouse by an armed Maasai warrior—which, of course, only added to the romance.

CHAPTER 15: AFRICA

That night we dined by candlelight in what's known as the boma, an outdoor circular enclosure, usually made of sticks and branches tightly knit together to keep wild animals out, and in honor of Valentine's Day, there was a big heart, in lights, hanging on the boma wall. My husband looked so handsome. His years of consistently going to the gym had paid off, and the T-shirt they gave him because our luggage hadn't arrived yet looked as good as any fancy shirt. And although Bill was just one month short of his fifty-ninth birthday, there wasn't a single gray in his luscious brown hair—amazing how God answered that seemingly shallow prayer for a man with dark brown hair. That night, snuggled in our treehouse under the mosquito net, we could hear an elephant trumpeting in the distance. It was the perfect start to a honeymoon that I had waited so long for, but now, the wait was over. It felt like God was smiling on us—and this was just the beginning.

Day 2

We were awakened by a knock at the door and a tray of some much-needed lattes. It was our first official day on safari, and we wanted to get an early start. After a heartier breakfast, we joined Freddy and headed out in the Jeep to Lake Manyara, where we hoped the animals would be gathering for a morning drink. As we approached the lake, we saw scores of baboons in a commotion, and then we saw why. A lioness was looking for an easy breakfast among the meaty primates. We witnessed a "lion kill," which, according to Fredy, is a rare sight, as they usually hunt at night. We watched as the lioness chased and captured the baboon and then carried it off by the neck somewhere to enjoy her snack. For my husband, Bill, a lifelong hunter and lover of all animals, being on safari was a dream come true. Bill took meticulous notes on every animal and bird we saw and wrote a beautiful memoir of our trip...here's an excerpt.

Bill Writing

I've always been an early riser, unlike Wendy, who prefers to sleep in, but we both were excited to start our first official day on safari. Hunting and animal sightings are always best early in the morning! That said, I hope I was successful in balancing some leisurely mornings, as it was our honeymoon, and we both wanted to soak it all in. Hot lattes were delivered by our server Trace at 6 a.m. as arranged, along with heart-shaped shortbread cookies—all so delicious! We gathered ourselves and put on the only clothes we had, ready for our first safari day (our luggage had not made the trip with us but was later delivered to the treehouse). Breakfast was outstanding, served in the open-air kitchen area overlooking the boma, and was a buffet of coffee, fresh juice, fresh fruit, crepes, eggs or omelets, and sweet treats. Thus fortified, we joined Fredy and began our adventure.

It was a short ride through the jungle to the shore of Lake Manyara. Leaving camp and driving in the jungle, I immediately saw a large number of obvious game trails and wondered what may have traveled them the night before. We didn't see any wild animals until the lake shore, where stood a few wildebeest and zebra. We later learned that these two species are friends and rarely travel without one another for reasons I'll explain later. The lake shimmered in the morning sun and was really quite beautiful. On the far side, perhaps a few miles away, stood distant mountains, which Fredy explained we had passed somewhere on the long journey in. I also saw my favorite ugly animal, a warthog, hanging out on the plain.

Then, as we drove north around a slow curve, I noticed dozens of baboons on the ground, running in our direction. Seconds later, I noticed zebras running away from us from the same area. About that time, Fredy accelerated and said, "Something is going on up here." I had the same thought—a predator. The baboons were the thing that really caught my eye, as perhaps a couple of hundred ran hard for cover. There really was nowhere to hide but one lone tree on the plain between us and the lake, and most of them made for it hastily. I saw dozens already up the tree and an equal number scrambling up a big branch on the right side. All the weight caused the branch to break, and those that couldn't jump off to another branch tumbled to the ground. I didn't really see the first lioness make her kill, but Fredy and Wendy did. I did see her carrying a limp baboon in her mouth and walking away from the tree back toward the road we were on.

We got great pictures from no more than fifteen yards away as she ate, loudly crunching bones and leaving no scraps. Being so green with the camera, I wasn't prepared to capture what happened next. I looked to my right and behind us to see a nice herd of Cape buffalo come out of the bush and onto the grassy plain to graze. Seeing this and apparently just warming up her appetite with the baboon, the lioness got up, took a low crouch, and made a bit of a charge at the buffalo. Alone, she was certainly no real threat, but they grouped up tightly anyway, moved the babies to the middle of the herd, and ran away a bit, then turned the tables and chased the lion back into the bush! All the while, Fredy screamed, "Video, video!" I got some good still shots of the mock lion charge but had to search for the video button on the camera. By the time I got to it, the lion was almost in the bush, but I recorded some of the buffalo stampede chasing her.

Fredy was very excited and told us in his eight years of game drives, that was the first kill he'd witnessed with clients. He opined that we must have a blessed marriage! Well, in a total of about one hour on safari, we had quite a morning! The buffalo returned from the bush, apparently satisfied the lion threat was gone, and moved back to the plain. We drove further on the same dirt road, observing some impala, various birds, flamingos, and an eagle, and stopped to take some nice zebra pictures.

We continued our drive and eventually came to a restroom (called a washroom by the Tanzanians). Wendy was in need of such a break and put aside her fear of a lion attack as we all visited the facilities. I got a short glimpse of a male bushbuck (thanks for the ID on that, Fredy!), a very shy reddish-brown creature, a bit bigger than our deer, with medium size horns. He didn't show much of himself or for long, but it was cool to see him. At this juncture, there was a long dock built out onto the lake, a perfect place to stretch one's legs and take some pictures. Many birds were in the area, including white heron, Egyptian geese, shorebirds, and some others who looked like purple martins. In the water a couple of hundred yards away were the hippos, only their backs exposed as before.

A Cape buffalo and her calf lounged and foraged in the muddy marsh area and paid no attention to us at all. There was a hot spring nearby that released very hot water, which ran to the lake in narrow creeks, spawning green algae grass to grow on the bottom and wave in the current. The marsh and small rocks surrounding the discharge were yellowed from the minerals coming out. We went to the hot spring and found the nearby rocks to be almost too warm to touch. The water itself bubbled out of the rocks, gave off mild steam, and really was too hot to touch! One could have made their morning coffee from that water straight out of the ground. Amazing!

Further down the road, we came around a curve and saw our first elephant! A decent bull with medium ivory, he had a mouth full of some vegetation and walked directly at the car. He didn't look mad but didn't look especially happy either. I just kept snapping pictures while Wendy asked if perhaps we should back up! Fredy said to just speak softly and we'd be fine. Sure enough, our buddy came within maybe a dozen yards of the car, then eased off to the left into the trees, but not before browsing on some more leaves and branches. As we moved away from the first guy, another elephant appeared, giving us a shorter round of photo ops before disappearing. We finalized our morning by looking at some hippos in a wooded pool by a concrete bridge. Again, they mostly stayed underwater, but I did get a few good pics as they moved around and partially revealed themselves. At least they were much closer than those we'd seen in the lake. Fredy pointed out that hippos always swish their tails when they defecate in the water. This helps spread the fertilizer and feeds the fish. Good trivia for future conversations! The remaining short ride to the treehouse was uneventful, but has there ever been a better first-morning safari?

Wendy Writes

After two unforgettable nights at our treehouse in Lake Manyara, we then ventured to the famous Ngorongoro Crater, a large volcanic caldera home to some thirty thousand animals, including around two dozen black rhino, which remain critically endangered. It's also home to the densest known lion population on the planet. After a night at a mountain lodge overlooking the Crater, where we thankfully saw the big five (lions, leopards, elephants, Cape buffalo, and rhino), it was time to get a little closer to nature. For the next two nights, the only thing separating Bill and me from the wild animals would be a cloth canvas.

When planning our adventure, I was highly encouraged not to miss the experience of staying in a tented camp, as this is when you feel most on "true safari." It was February, and the wildebeest migration was in full swing in the Serengeti. Every year, about two million wildebeest, zebra, and gazelle move in a constant journey that takes them across the Masai Mara plains in Kenya, all the way south into Tanzania's Serengeti and then back again—in search of greener pastures. The annual migration northwest, at the end of the rainy season (usually May or June), according to National Geographic, is recognized as one of the "seven wonders of the natural world." When we arrived at our camp, they showed us to our tent, which, thankfully looked more like a small tan house and came with a full, working bathroom, including a hot shower. When you were ready for your shower, you let the staff know, and they would come and pour the hot water in a tank for you, and amazingly, it was always the right amount. They also showed us a horn next to the bed that we could blow should any of the predators lurking at night get too close. A little unnerving, but we were assured those unwanted advances were rare, plus we wanted the full safari experience!

That first night, the wildebeest were so close to our tent we could hear them grunting and stomping loudly through our canvas walls, which made falling asleep a bit challenging, but there'd be time for sleeping later. Bill also heard a lion roar in the distance, which I thankfully did not. In the morning, we watched in amazement as hundreds of wildebeest and zebra marched past our tent. I was sure I saw a lion amongst the throng of wildebeest, but Bill finally convinced me it was just a large tan-colored antelope. Later that day, in the Jeep, we came across an amazing lion kill. About seven or eight female lions and a couple of males surrounded a large antelope they had taken down. From the looks of things, the lions had already filled their bellies and were now just guarding the remains from the hyenas that were waiting impatiently nearby to finish the leftovers. It had been another incredible day on safari, and I thanked God that we had chosen Africa for our honeymoon destination. In the evenings, after dinner, we sat around a fire with fellow guests to watch "bush

TV," as the locals called it. No need for television on safari; watching the animals in the distance while the golden African sun set on the Serengeti was enchanting all by itself.

After surviving the "tented camp" experience, which, when I go back, I will definitely do again, we decided to end our time in Africa with a little luxury. We loaded up the Jeep and headed for the sumptuous Four Seasons Serengeti. The four-hour Jeep ride allowed us to take in even more of the sweeping Serengeti.

When we arrived, we were greeted with champagne on ice and designer chocolates and escorted to our special honeymoon room that overlooked the infinity pool and a pond frequented by a family of elephants. The maître d' informed us that the elephants had already visited the pond and would probably not be back today. Not wanting to miss this, I grabbed Bill's hand and prayed, "Lord, please send the elephants back today!" Not a few minutes later, as we stood on our hotel balcony overlooking the vast African plains, I screamed! "Bill, the elephants are coming back!" At least eight of them, from the papa to the mama to what looked like several teenagers, maybe some aunts and uncles and a couple of babies, slowly marched back to the pond to drink. We snapped dozens of pictures and watched as the family finally had their fill and meandered back further onto the plains until they were out of sight.

After the long Jeep ride, Bill and I decided to take a dip in the pool. We thought it sure would have been nice to be in the pool when the elephants arrived because the pool and the pond were so close. Amazingly, as if on cue, the family of elephants returned to the pond!

They must have been really thirsty! God was showing off and giving us even the small desires of our hearts to be near the elephants.

What I didn't know then is that Bill had a serious collection of safari and African hunting books, everything from *Death in the Long Grass* by Peter Hathaway Capstick to *The Horn of the Hunter* by the famous American hunter and writer Robert Ruark—at least fifty of them in a wooden chest in his house back in Virginia. It wasn't until we got home from our honeymoon that I discovered this incredible cache of books on Africa in his uncle's WW2 chest. "Honey!" I yelled. "You have so many books on Africa! Why didn't you tell me? You must have always wanted to go there!" "Yes," he said, "but I never thought it would be possible until I met you."

When God brings the right person into your life, He gives you even the deep desires of your heart and helps you achieve dreams you never thought possible on your own. Now, we're already dreaming of our next African adventure. Who says it needs to be a once-in-a-lifetime trip? I've been several times. Africa never actually leaves you anyway—and is always beckoning until you return to her.

16

Married Living Separately

"For this reason, a man shall leave his father and mother and be joined to his wife, and the two shall become one flesh'; so then they are no longer two, but one flesh."

Mark 10:7–8

When we arrived home from our honeymoon, we had to decide: where do we live? We both still owned our own individual homes. I had a three-story condo that I had lived in for fifteen years, and he had a condo down by the beach that he bought when he was in his twenties and later rented but had returned to after his divorce. I loved Bill's place, a quintessential bachelor pad with honey-colored hardwood floors that Bill had put in himself, a wood-burning fireplace (the only kind you should have, in my opinion), a deer head mounted over the fireplace, and a large white marlin mounted over the couch that was so deep you could get lost in it. There were hunting and fishing magazines neatly stacked on the end tables as well as fishing trophies and a large-mounted citation flounder on the wall—the biggest he'd ever caught. After dating a few guys who were more in touch with their feminine side, it was refreshingly manly. And with two bedrooms and two full baths, it was comfy and cozy, but it wouldn't become home anytime soon.

My condo, about thirty miles away (Bill always joked that I lived in the western part of the state because it was such a long drive), was in pretty good shape but needed some updating before I could put it on the market. Fortunately, Bill worked in construction while in college and is very skilled at putting in flooring, mending and painting decks, and more. After putting all new stainless-steel appliances and new flooring in the kitchen, upgrading the tile in two bathrooms, and fixing the deck, my condo was ready to sell.

During this time, Bill and I were going back and forth to each other's homes, which was kind of fun and felt like we were still dating, but there were still plenty of nights I was by myself. I remember thinking that God was giving me time to transition into marriage—into being with another human being twenty-four seven, 365 days a year! After fifty-four and a half years of being single, of being on my own, God knew that I needed this "transition time." Yes, we could have tried to do all of this before we got married, but that would have taken several more months, and neither of us wanted to wait; plus, God was now using it to help us both ease into this new life—marriage, the two becoming one, and everything that entails.

We had an amazing realtor, Janice, who helped me stage my condo perfectly and got me top dollar! It sold quickly, and finally, after six months of going back and forth—I was officially moving in with Bill! And I was ready. After fifteen years in one place—I was so ready to say goodbye to not just a condo and a neighborhood but to a way of life. When I drove away after cleaning every square inch of that condo, it was a sweet parting. I said goodbye with a heart full of gratitude to God for giving me a safe place to live and thankfulness for the years of His grace to help me wait for this day. I prayed the next owner would feel God's peace and presence and be as blessed there as I was.

Living under One Roof

Once I left my old neighborhood, I never looked back. God's timing is so perfect that I didn't miss it one tiny bit. Now though, if Bill and I got into a disagreement, which was extremely rare, I couldn't run back to my condo and to what my husband jokingly refers to as my "pothole"—I had slept on one side of the bed for so long that my mattress developed a "pothole." Even now he likes to kid me and ask me if I miss my "pothole," which—trust me—I do not! I love being married more than I ever dreamed I would, and when Bill is out of town, I don't sleep as well because I'm so used to him being there now.

After a few months of just enjoying being under one roof, it was time to now work on Bill's condo. It didn't need quite as many repairs or upgrades as my place did, and we were able to put it on the market in March of 2020—which, by the way, is when the coronavirus pandemic erupted. But Janice worked her magic, and once again, it sold quickly and at top dollar. God was making a way for us to have a real house—and, more importantly, be closer to Bill's elderly parents. And after more than three decades, Bill was ready to say goodbye to his condo too. It was a little too cramped for us—especially since we were also living with Bill's two beagle dogs. We both desperately wanted a real house with a backyard, and God was about to give us the desires of our heart—even during a pandemic.

Coming Home

Bill was raised on an island in Virginia Beach—in the same house his parents bought in 1954, years before he was born. He grew up on the water, and that's where he feels at home. While we were dating, a house in that neighborhood was for sale, and I thought it would be perfect for us. Only trouble was we weren't even engaged yet, so the point was mute. Meanwhile, Janice, our relator extraordinaire, had shown us at least thirty homes in and around the area, but nothing felt quite right.

Divine Timing

About the same time Bill's condo sold to a nice young man in his twenties, that house I had admired in Bill's old neighborhood went back on the market! I couldn't believe the timing. Janice immediately got us an appointment, and we checked it out. Fortunately, a Navy SEAL who had owned it a few years back had given it a marvelous makeover and literally raised the roof, so it had the vaulted ceilings that I had come to love as well as an island in the kitchen that was as big as our former kitchen. Even better, it was practically across the street from Bill's parents. We could see their house from the window.

It wasn't a perfect house, but it was perfect for us. We moved in thirty days later. Little did we know then, although we should have, what a blessing it would be to be so close to Bill's parents. Bill's dad, George, a WW2 vet, lived to be one hundred and was just three months shy of his 101st birthday when he passed. And as of this writing, his mother, Thelma, a WW2 nurse, is still going strong at 102, and we see her every day. Not a day goes by that we don't thank God for allowing us to be this close to Thelma and in a neighborhood that we really love and enjoy.

Although we didn't do it the way most couples do—get married and then immediately move into a house together—we did it our way. And I believe for us it was the best way. God is writing your story, and it's a unique story based on your unique journey and how God made you, and it doesn't have to look like everyone else's story.

One more little God-wink about the house we're living in now. When Bill was growing up, his parents were very good friends with a couple that lived in this house, Jake and Mary. They made many fun memories at each other's homes, cooking out, laughing, and hosting parties. Jake and Mary did not have children of their own, and they loved Bill. When Mary passed, she remembered Bill in her will. We think Mary and Jake would be tickled knowing that Bill and I are so happy in their former home.

17

What's For Dinner?

"Food is a love language, one most of us speak."

—Sarah Copeland

If you're married, you already know this is the most important question of the day—if you're not married yet, you need to understand it will be. When Bill and I first got married, I didn't understand what felt like my husband's obsession with the evening meal. You just eat when you're hungry, and you don't worry about it, right? Ha! Those days of take-out on the run or a lean cuisine with a pint of Ben & Jerry's to follow are long gone. I know that wasn't the healthiest, but I was working out a bit more and apparently burning off the calories.

Suffice it to say, I have evolved since then and am happier for it, although still learning that food and especially the dinner meal can equate to love in your husband's eyes. Yes, it's an old saying, but there's a lot of truth in it—*the way to a man's heart is through his stomach.*

When Bill and I were dating, he came over to my condo one chilly November evening during deer hunting season after sitting in a tree stand all day, and I surprised him by making a chicken pot pie from scratch (except for the crust, which was Pillsbury). Bill still talks about that chicken pot pie to this day as if it was the most delicious meal he's ever had. It was actually the first time I made it too! And yes, I still love making it for him, but that day was special because he'd been outside hunting all day, he was hungry and tired, and he came home to a hot cooked meal prepared by his woman. I still remember the way he smelled that night when I hugged him; he was dressed in camo and smelled just like the woods! Trust me, it was better than any cologne, and I was happy to make my man a good hot meal that he enjoyed.

Bill is an excellent chef, and I really enjoy watching him cook because he has such an ease in the kitchen and makes everything look like art. I especially love when he brings me breakfast in bed—if dinner makes him feel loved, breakfast in bed makes me feel loved and a bit like a queen! We also like to cook together and enjoy an occasional dinner date out at one of our favorite restaurants, but suffice it to say, most men love it when you cook for them.

When we were dating and first married, I only had a couple of entrée dishes I felt confident about—my beef stew and my chicken soup. I knew these were winners—at least in my book, they were— but you can only make beef stew so many times before your "favorite" becomes a little too familiar. Fortunately, Bill and I both love fish and could eat it almost every night and often do during the summer months. So I quickly learned to prepare fish the way he did in his big black iron skillet with unsalted butter (to keep it from burning at high heat) and a good blackened seasoning—it's a winner every time. Serve it with a side of broccoli or asparagus and a sweet potato, and you have a healthy and delicious dinner.

> *"All you need is love. But a little chocolate now and then doesn't hurt."*
>
> —Charles M. Schulz

My husband and I both love chocolate, and one of my favorite gifts that we received for our wedding was *The Newlywed Cookbook* by Sarah Copeland. In this amazing cookbook, where she also shares her fascinating love story with her husband, Andras, there is a chocolate layer cake recipe called "Better-than-Boxed Chocolate Cake" that is, in my opinion, the best homemade chocolate cake that I have ever made and that my husband simply adores. If you like a rich chocolate cake that's not too sweet, you'll love this recipe as well. Birthdays and holidays, Bill always requests this chocolate cake, and I love to make it for him.

Copeland understood that preparing food for her husband was not just an act of love and a way to sustain life, but it was the best part of life. She wrote:

> *There's a moment in marriage, whether two days of two hundred and twenty-two days into it, where you're standing side by side in the morning barefoot on the cool kitchen floor. Everything is quiet but the hum of him making you coffee just the way you like it, with all that frothy milk and sugar. You're stirring together his favorite pancakes, sprinkling a*

few blueberries in the batter, and then it hits you, these simple moments are the best in life.

I couldn't agree more.

Bill's Words

I (Bill) am a product of my childhood environment. We were not rich by any means, and both my parents worked hard to make ends meet. My mother was a registered nurse and sometimes worked long and unusual hours. But one thing was a constant at our house—no matter the circumstances, dinner was on the table at 6 p.m. And Mom was the cook. She inherited her talent from my grandmother, who died when I was young but delivered lasting memories of her kitchen. She lived on a small farm in Massachusetts, and when she cooked, *she cooked*. I kind of think she was always cooking. I recall two or three different types of vegetables, meat, and potatoes at every meal. We all liked seafood, and I developed my reputation for eating my weight in soft shell "steamer" clams while standing at her stove. Dinner there was a literal "groaning board" of food, meaning the table groaned from the weight of it all. If your plate got low on anything, you'd better duck, as Nana would be right behind you with a long-handled spoon and slap another heaping helping on!

My mother became a good cook out of necessity. Dad was an Illinois farm boy, and dinner to him meant meat and potatoes. The man regarded rice and ethnic foods as light food for fairies. He'd have likely thrown a taco out the window. He did like shrimp, fish, and other seafood, but a carb and vegetable had to go with it. Dad was not one to help in the kitchen other than doing the dishes in his retirement years. Poor Mom struggled to get home and prepare the meal, and I don't ever recall her missing the 6 p.m. deadline. I don't know how she did it!

So naturally, as an adult, I think dinner should be served at 6 p.m. every night. Just kidding! It's totally irrational in this modern world because, most nights, I don't get home until after six, and often Wendy is working late as well. But somehow, maybe it's just the nostalgia of it and the wonderful memories of my mom and grandmother in the kitchen, but if we lived in a perfect world, yeah, dinner would still be on the table at 6 p.m. Perhaps we need to hire a chef!

As Wendy mentioned, we both do some cooking, and I really enjoy it as long as I'm not too rushed. I can piddle in the kitchen for quite a while. Wendy is a good cook, but she tends to want to get it over with and move on to more productive things like Netflix. She is more of a "recipe" cook and follows the ingredient list and measurements carefully. I tend to just throw stuff in the pan or pot and let it rip. She asks me silly questions like, "How much basil or red pepper did you add?" or "Did you use a full teaspoon of salt?" Sometimes she even wants to know how long I cooked something. The answer to that one is always "until it's done"! I use recipes as guidelines or suggestions and just do my own thing. I like to think I'm creative! Most of the time, it works, but sometimes I just blow it.

When we were dating, we visited Wendy's brother Pete and his family. I promised to make my famous blueberry pancakes for everyone for breakfast. I even had a cute little helper in the form of her niece, Keaton, who helped stir the batter. I did it from memory, not the recipe, and the pancakes were horrible! In fact, I'm still trying to live that one down, as Wendy just rolls her eyes when I suggest pancakes made from scratch. I'm usually in charge of the meat component of the dinner, especially if it involves grilling. Most men enjoy cooking more if there's an element of danger. Some missing hair on your arm or a singed eyebrow is a small price to pay for a properly grilled steak.

As much as I do enjoy cooking when I have time, nothing, I repeat *almost nothing*, is better than your wife making you a good home-cooked meal (with that special Better-than-Boxed Chocolate Cake!). It's ten times better after a long day in the field or on the boat fishing. In fact, I believe there are few marital issues that can't be resolved in this fashion! So some advice to the loved one here, be you male or female: learn how to cook. Experiment, collaborate, be adventurous, and try new things. You'll find out what you both like. It's best when you enjoy cooking together, but equally good when either of you can put a meal on the table when needed on a given evening.

We prefer to eat a generally healthy diet, and good food costs more than unhealthy food. I love fresh things I catch, shoot, or harvest from the garden or maybe the neighbor's fig tree. In the summer, Wendy and I enjoy walking out to our small garden and surveying the tomatoes, cucumbers, squash, basil, and other herbs we're growing. We both love "living off the land" as much as possible—even if it's just making fresh pesto from the basil you picked or enjoying a juicy tomato sandwich. There's nothing like the taste of a home-grown tomato. We also believe in the "buy local" philosophy and regularly buy local shrimp, oysters, sausage, fruit, and more. The Bible implores us to enjoy our food and drink—for it is a good reward for our labor. Ecclesiastes 8:15.

For certain, one of the best things in life is sitting down to a healthy, delicious dinner with the one you love. I really can't think of anything better—unless, of course, there's chocolate cake.

18

You Gotta Belize It—Again!

"And we know that all things work together for good to those who love God, to those who are the called according to His purpose."

Romans 8:28

The last time I was blessed to step foot on this particular piece of sandy paradise, I was in the worst heartbreak of my life. The man I thought God had for me had suddenly and without warning (except for the red flags I ignored) broken up with me and broken my heart.

As you may recall from my previous book, *You Are a Prize to Be Won,* and the chapter "You Gotta Belize It," I sought solace on the island (actually the peninsula) of San Pedro, Belize, for two weeks hoping to return not only tan and healthy but, by some miracle, healed of my heartbreak. That did not happen—although it was the best tan and the best snorkeling of my life. However, the heartbreak lasted for much longer than I ever dreamed possible.

Fast forward ten years later—February 2022. My husband Bill and I decided to take a quick romantic getaway for our third wedding anniversary. We celebrated our first wedding anniversary two years earlier at a Sandals Resort in Negril, Jamaica! I had never done an all-inclusive, and it was just what we needed—sun, sand, paddle boarding, water skiing, and a variety of restaurants to choose from every evening. The breakfasts were my favorite, though. We dined al fresco overlooking the cove and the still blue water while the sea birds kept my husband well entertained. We filled up on fresh papaya, eggs, and pastries, and the best part was when the waiters would come around with a silver pitcher and say in a gorgeous island accent, "Would you like some Jamaican Blue Mountain coffee?" The answer was always yes, and with a little cream, it was the perfect way to wake up in paradise. Not far away, we visited the famous Rick's Café, where you are guaranteed the most unforgettable views of the sun sinking into the sea as well as the breathtaking spectacle of watching the locals and a few brave tourists jump from cliffs as high as forty feet! Most opt for the lower cliffs—the lowest ledge is about eight feet. Bill couldn't resist and took the plunge, but thankfully from a much lower perch. I, of course, caught it all on video.

The following year, the COVID-19 pandemic had pretty much shut down air travel, so we staycationed for our second anniversary at a beachfront hotel about twenty minutes from our home. Yes, it was February, one of the coldest months in Virginia Beach, but we still enjoyed a change of scenery and a walk on the beach, even if it was a bit chilly.

By early 2022, with the pandemic somewhat under control, we decided it was time to travel again for our third anniversary. We were thinking of going to Phoenix to hike Camelback Mountain, but then a friend mentioned Belize. Turns out Belize was a lot less expensive than Phoenix, and I was able to use some frequent flyer miles I had earned, so it was off to Belize and a little island called Caye Caulker. The motto on Caye Caulker is "go slow," and that was music to my husband's ears, as we had both been burning the candle at both ends and needed a vacay—even if it was only for four nights.

Back in 2012, I had made a day trip to explore Caye Caulker, a tiny island about a thirty-minute ferry ride from San Pedro. Caye Caulker is easy to explore, as it's only about five miles long and less than a mile wide, surrounded by the most gorgeous clear turquoise water I've ever seen. That day, just before our boat was about to head back to San Pedro, I darted into a little art store and immediately fell in love with this original acrylic painting of two toucan birds in the jungle. Their bright yellow faces with fuchsia and orange bills were so happy, I just had to have it. I desperately needed some happy in my life.

Over the years, that painting, which hung in various places in my condo when I was single and now hangs in our kitchen, has given me so much joy that I decided to contact the artist, Debbie Cooper, to see if she was still painting on the island. My hope was to buy another tropical painting to add to my "happy" collection. Turns out Debbie and her husband, Bruce, had closed their shop and moved back to the States, but by "chance" she was going to be on Caye Caulker at the same time Bill and I would be there, and she was bringing some original paintings with her!

I was thrilled at the chance of finally meeting her face to face and, of course, hopefully gaining a new piece of art to cherish, but mostly to let her know how much her painting had meant to me over the years. I also wanted to give her my book because I had written about her colorful toucans and their "happy" effect on me in chapter 5, "You Gotta Belize It."

Caye Caulker is a small and friendly island, and it didn't take long before we discovered where she and her husband were staying—the hotel right next to Bill and me!

As we approached, Debbie put out her cigarette and stood up. She was a small, tan lady, probably in her sixties, with short blonde hair. After our hellos, she showed me some of her new paintings, and I selected a couple of pieces. After a brief chat, I asked if we could take a photo together. I held a new colorful canvas depicting a bright orange papaya, my favorite tropical fruit, that I bought from her (which looks great in my kitchen, by the way), and she held my book in her hands. But before my husband could even snap the photo, I started to cry.

Full-Circle Moment

The tears caught me and, I'm sure, Debbie totally by surprise. It was a full-circle moment. The pain I'd felt the last time I was on this island was long gone—and now, here I was, back on Caye Caulker, but this time, celebrating my wedding anniversary with my amazing husband of three years and getting to meet the artist whose painting was a prophetic promise of happier days to come.

Debbie is so humble that I'm not sure she quite understood how impactful her art was and is, although I did my best to let her know and to thank her for it. Perhaps my tears said more than my words could ever convey. After the photo, we hugged, and I simply said, "God is using you." "That makes me happy," she said smiling. I thought, *If this is the only reason we're here on this remote little island off the coast of Belize, then this moment was worth it.* My husband was also moved by meeting the artist who meant so much to me. One of my favorite scriptures, Joel 2:25, was coming to life, "*So I will restore to you the years that the swarming locust has eaten.*" God was indeed restoring the years.

The next few days were a blur of morning walks to our favorite coffee hut for iced lattes on the beach, grilled sweet Caribbean spiny lobster for lunch, red or yellow snapper for dinner, and making sure we were in the perfect spot every evening to watch the famous Caribbean sunset.

The last time I was on Caye Caulker, it took all of my faith to believe Romans 8:28 was true—that somehow, God could use my heartbreak for good. I remember saying it out loud over and over like a mantra, "And we know that all things work together for good to those who love God and are called according to His purpose." If I'd only known that God was going to take that pain and birth a book that has been a lifeline and encouragement to so many women and then, later, let me meet the perfect man for me. Not perfect but perfect for me. But God doesn't tell us everything; otherwise, we wouldn't need faith—He only lights the path right in front of us and asks us to trust Him.

God told me, "This season (of pain) will end"—and it did. And if you're going through heartbreak or even just weary from the waiting, hold on! Brighter days are just around the corner. I encourage you to do something that makes you happy or perhaps buy a piece of art like I did (doesn't have to be expensive), but just something that makes you happy—to encourage yourself that better days are coming! Happy is coming!

Although our trip to Caye Caulker was short, it was a sweet time of celebrating three years of being in love. Marriage, like singleness, is a gift to be celebrated. And yes, you can celebrate closer to home, but if you enjoy traveling, which I do, then you can combine your love for adventure with your special someone or go solo like I did when I was single—I never let being single stop me from traveling or being adventurous.

We ran into Debbie and Bruce one more time before we left and got to say goodbye, although I told her I still might need one more painting from her in the future. By the way, if you're even visiting Caye Caulker, several of the art stores still carry some of her work—which to me, captures the beauty, the color, and the joy of the tropics and, for a once heartbroken single girl, the promise of happier days ahead.

You didn't miss it!

19

Your Wait Is Not in Vain

Waiting! Yes, waiting! Still waiting!
The Master will not be late:
Since He knows that I am waiting
For Him to unlatch the gate.

—J. Danson Smith

I'm not an expert on marriage, having only been married for several years; however, I am an expert on waiting. And I'm here to testify that God is faithful in the waiting. He is the God who fulfills His promises to those who believe. I read the above poem in my beloved *Streams in the Desert* devotional that I reread every year, but in May of 2016, about a year before I met my future husband, I wrote underneath those words, "Yes, Lord! You will do this for me!" And He did. In His perfect timing, God unlatched the gate of years and years of waiting. And God will do it for you as well.

If you're in a season of waiting on God for something or someone—like I was—you need to know that *God has not forgotten you.* He hears your prayers—He listens to the cry of your heart, and He will answer you.

In Psalm 98 God says, *"He has remembered His mercy and His faithfulness to the house of Israel."* (Insert your own name here.)

The Bible says, *"Delight yourself in the Lord and He will give you the desires of your heart"* (Psalm 37:4). But it also says, *"Wait patiently for the Lord! Be brave and courageous. Yes, wait for the Lord!"* (Psalm 27:14, NLT).

Why is it so important to wait? Because there's *purpose* in the waiting.

Waiting, although not pleasant, has many benefits, according to the Bible, including:

— Those who wait on the Lord will renew their strength! Isaiah 40:31

— Those who wait on the Lord will not be ashamed! Psalm 25:3

— And those who wait on the Lord will not be disappointed! Isaiah 43:23

Also, you don't get a testimony without a test!

My test was waiting. And if you are reading this book, I'm guessing it's probably your test as well. But if you stay in faith, I know it's a test you will pass with ultimately a great story to tell.

God Is Never Late

God is never late. He's rarely early, but He's always right on time! God has appointed times and seasons for us—but thankfully, He often lets us know when we're getting close!

For example, it was a long wait for Abraham and Sarah, who were promised a son, but when the time was getting close, God sent three travelers to deliver a message to Abraham, a message that must have been very sweet to his ears.

> *Then one of them said, "I will surely return to you about this time next year, and Sarah your wife will have a son."*
>
> *Now Sarah was listening at the entrance to the tent, which was behind him. Abraham and Sarah were already very old, and Sarah was past the age of childbearing. So Sarah laughed to herself as she thought, "After I am worn out and my lord is old, will I now have this pleasure?"*
>
> *Then the LORD said to Abraham, "Why did Sarah laugh and say, 'Will I really have a child, now that I am old?' Is anything too hard for the LORD? I will return to you at the appointed time next year, and Sarah will have a son."*
>
> Genesis 18:10–14 (NIV)

God spoke the same message to the Shunamite woman through the prophet Elisha in 2 Kings chapter 4.

> *Say now to her, "Look, you have been concerned for us with all this care. What can I do for you? Do you want me to*

speak on your behalf to the king or to the commander of the
army?"

She answered, "I dwell among my own people."

So he said, "What then is to be done for her?"

And Gehazi answered, "Actually, she has no son, and her
husband is old."

So he said, "Call her." When he had called her, she stood in
the doorway. Then he said, "About this time next year you
shall embrace a son."

And she said, "No, my lord. Man of God, do not lie to your
maidservant!"

But the woman conceived and bore a son when the appoint-
ed time had come, of which Elisha had told her.

2 Kings 4:13–17

God is merciful in that He doesn't tell us *how long* we'll have to
wait, but He does clue us in when the time of fulfillment is near.

God did this for me as well. He sent a stranger I had never met
through a series of letters and a special gift of a wedding frame where
he said my picture would soon go to let me know that God was about
to bring "the one" I had been praying for. I was a bit skeptical at first,
just like Sarah had been, but as time passed, I knew that this person
was sent from God to let me know that the time of fulfillment was
drawing near.

It's when we're almost at the finish line that it's often the hardest
to keep going! But we gain strength from those who are cheering us

on and from those who have gone before us, saying, "You're so close! Hang in there! The wait is almost over!"

The Wait Is Over

On February 9th, 2019, to be exact, my wait was finally over. God answered what had been the predominant and constant prayer of my life! And at the age of fifty-four, I became a bride.

It was the fulfillment of years of waiting, watching, and wondering:

— who God would bring into my life,

— when He would do it, and

— how He would do it.

I had a lot of questions, and the only thing I kept hearing over and over from the Lord was—*wait.*

The good news is—*due season does come!* Psalm 102:13 says, "*You will arise and have mercy on Zion; [insert your name] for the time to favor her, yes, the set time, [the appointed time,] has come.*" I believe there was an appointed time for me to meet Bill—yes, the waiting was long and hard, but I can testify now that my husband was worth the wait and that God's timing really is perfect!

I'm a late bloomer. I was a late bloomer physically and a late bloomer emotionally—I also had a lot of "stuff" I needed to get healed from before I was ready to be married. Plus, my broadcasting career really took off when I turned forty, and I was having the time of my life reporting from danger zones and international hot spots around the world. I wouldn't have wanted to miss this for anything.

God had wired me for this kind of adventure, and if I had been married or had children at the time, that dream may not have been fulfilled.

Your Wait Is Not in Vain

As I said before, I think it's worth repeating there is purpose in your waiting. God doesn't ever make us wait to punish us—only to protect us, prepare us, and make us ready for the incredible blessings He wants to bestow on us.

Isaiah 30:18 says, "*Therefore the Lord will wait, that He may be gracious to you; and therefore, He will be exalted, that He may have mercy on you...Blessed are all those who wait for Him.*"

Worth the Wait

Now, I don't know what you're waiting for—it may not be a husband; it may be a dream job or a baby or a loved one's salvation or something else, but if it is a husband, you may be saying, "I sure hope I don't have to wait as long as Wendy did!" I get it, and don't worry—your story is unique, and God will not require you to wait one day longer than is absolutely necessary to bless you with your heart's desires.

Your Story Doesn't Have to Look Like Everyone Else's

As I mentioned before, one day I was praying in my prayer loft, asking the Lord, once again, "Where is my husband?" I heard the Holy

Spirit whisper, "When you're ready, there he will be." I was astonished at what I had just heard. I had already had my fiftieth birthday, and the Lord was telling me that I wasn't quite ready yet! I was tempted to argue with the Lord, and actually, I'm pretty sure I did, but in these cases, God is always right because He knows us better than we know ourselves. However, with this priceless bit of information, I could be confident in knowing that God was at work—and apparently, I still had some work to do as well to get ready for the blessing of marriage.

God Will Restore the Years

Although the waiting seemed long at the time, I can honestly say God has erased the pain of those lonely years of waiting. Joel 2:25–26 says, "*God will restore the years that the locusts ate.*" God has a way of making up for lost time.

You're Closer than You Think

I believe you're so much closer than you think. The enemy of our souls would love for you to give up and settle for less than God has for you. Don't do it! You're closer than you think, and God is hearing every precious prayer you're praying and saving all of your salty tears in a bottle (liquid prayers). Your faith and your courage to keep waiting on God's best is not easy, but God is faithful, and He will not disappoint you if you don't give up.

Hebrews 10:23 says, "*Let us hold unswervingly to the hope we profess for He who promised is faithful.*" God is faithful and will do all that He has promised you and more. Right now, He's working behind the scenes, lining things up for you and preparing you for your blessing. If God, who has placed the sun and the moon and the stars in their perfect place in the heavens and even calls the stars by name (Psalm 147:4), can run the universe, how much more can He order the circumstances in your life to bring you into perfect alignment with your future spouse or whatever you're waiting for?

Keep believing, keep praying, and keep hoping because, in His perfect time, the stars will align, and your prayers will suddenly be answered, just like they were for me.

You didn't miss it!

20

Jemimah's Story

"'Not by might, nor by power, but by My spirit,' says the Lord of hosts"
(Zechariah 4:6).
"God will do it! You just have to let go."

—Jemimah

This next story is from my dear friend Jemimah, who I met on Instagram a few years ago when she was single and reading my book *You Are a Prize to Be Won.* She was struggling in the waiting and knew that I could relate. Although she said I encouraged her, Jemimah encouraged me, now that I was married, to write about meeting my husband and also to do more on social media. Sorry, Jemimah, still need help with social media—but I did follow your advice to write this book!

Jemimah, who is from England and now lives in South Africa, has a beautiful love story that could be a movie. I know you will love it as much as I do.

"He Wrote the Story"

In 2018 I was reading Wendy's book *You Are a Prize to Be Won*. It encouraged me deeply and gave me strength to move on from a very damaging friendship. Wendy's faith increased my own faith that God would fulfill His promise and bring me a husband. I had just turned forty. In the previous twenty years, I had seen God move powerfully in my life, guiding me into a career as a journalist, traveling the world, and writing biographies, but in the area of love, I experienced disappointment and heartbreak.

When I was in my late thirties, living in London, single and aware that forty was fast approaching (which psychologically felt like a cut-off point of being "too late"), I had a dream.

In the dream, I was standing in front of a big steel, immovable door. It was massive, and I was trying everything in my own strength to open it, but it would not budge. Eventually I gave up and, despondent, sat on the ground with my back to the door. I then woke up. The feeling of frustration was still so present. "This is what it feels like to find a husband and get married," I told God as I got out of bed. "It's impossible."

I went on with my day, but that evening I went to a worship night at a friend's house. A girl said she had a word for someone in the room. She said, "I have a picture of a big steel immovable door. You have tried everything in your own strength to open it, and it's impossible. God says, 'It's not by might; it's not by power; it's by My spirit.' He will do it; you just have to let go" (Zechariah 4:6).

I was astounded. The girl had described the exact door I had seen in my dream, and God had spoken into my situation for what felt like the first time.

The next day I opened an email devotional. The text said, "God will open the door; you don't need to do anything."

For the next year, I got so many words and pictures from random people about a door that God was going to open, and it would be quick and easy...but nothing happened.

I tried to hold on to faith and reminded myself of Hebrews 11:1, "*Now faith is the substance of things hoped for, the evidence of things not seen.*" I decided to do something in faith: to believe the word God had spoken—that it was not my might or power but His Spirit who was going to bring us together. So I went out and bought a man's blue linen shirt...for my future husband! I hung it on the wall in my tiny bedroom in London to remind myself that God was going to bring him. But as the years went by, it felt like the shirt was taunting me, as nothing seemed to be happening!

About four years later, COVID arrived, and I left London to go to Norfolk (about a three-hour drive away) and stay with my parents. My dad had prostate cancer. He was an evangelist as well as a businessman, and he was so frustrated with lockdown—not being able to tell people about Jesus! So one day I decided to put him on Instagram. I started a page for him called "Walking as Jesus Walked" and filmed him sharing one-minute testimonies.

In the autumn his illness progressed, and he had to go into hospice. I visited him a week before he died, and although he could hardly speak, he said the first thing he was going to ask Jesus when he got to heaven was to bring my husband. I knew something was going to shift.

Dad went to be with Jesus in November 2021. He was eighty-six. I had always been afraid of being single and alone when he died, but when he eventually did go, amazingly, I felt the closeness and comfort of Jesus. I remember going for a walk the next day and telling Jesus I was okay! I felt Him say, "A man will always let you down, but I will never let you down." I knew at that point I did not need to get married. I wanted to, but if I didn't, I would be all right. Jesus really was sufficient.

I had been going for walks every day of lockdown, and my prayer had become, "Lord, I surrender to Your story; let my life give You glory."

It's cheesy because it rhymes, but I came to the point of realizing I had been fighting to write my own story, and it hadn't worked. My job as a journalist and author is to write other people's stories. I write missionary biographies, and I *know* that the best stories are those of people who have surrendered to God and let Him have His way in their life.

In January 2021 I was at home with Mum, and I really wondered what God was going to do. I was forty-three, sleeping in my childhood bedroom (which looked the same as when I was a teenager). We were snowed in and had run out of oil, so we had no heat. It was lockdown, so my grieving Mum could not see anyone; the telephone had broken, and everything looked bleak. One morning I was sitting reading my Bible and praying, asking God for hope!

Suddenly I felt Him speak twice about a husband, "He is coming in spring and coming from Africa."

However, I did not jump up and down with joy when I heard this. I got cross. I'd had the word about the door five years previously, and nothing had happened. I didn't want to hold on to another word and be disappointed.

Also, maybe He meant spring 2052...the words had not been for a specific year. I felt like the Shunammite woman in 2 Kings 4 when Elisha tells her in a year she will have a son. She was childless, and this must have been the deepest desire of her heart. When Elisha told her, she said, "Don't say that!" She feared disappointment and was afraid to hope. I felt the same, but I wrote the words in my journal and then forgot about them.

At the same time, I felt like I was supposed to continue my dad's Instagram and tell my own testimony. For ten weeks in early 2021, I uploaded a new video of me telling my story each Sunday.

On Monday, April 17th, 2021, I woke up in the middle of the night and heard the words, "Transition, transition, transition is coming!"

I didn't know what it meant, but the next morning I wrote it in my journal. Two days later Alister got in contact via my dad's Instagram. He rarely uses Instagram but had started watching my videos. He wondered whether I was the one God had for him but did not want to pursue something God was not in. He put out a fleece and posted a picture of some beautiful white flowers; if I commented, he would respond. I did, and he did.

Alister lives in Cape Town, where I had lived eighteen years previously. We have many friends in common, but we never actually met when I lived there. We started talking on the phone and spoke every day for hours at a time for two months.

I knew we had to meet just to be sure this was something we wanted to pursue. It was not easy, as because of COVID South Africa was on the UK red list, but all the doors opened for us—it was easy. I was able to stay with a dear friend who lived ten minutes from Alister and was also able to work from there. I stayed for nearly two months. One Saturday in July, Alister took me on a hike up a mountain, and when we got to the top, he asked me to be his wife. We married on October 23rd, six months after first being in contact.

It was then I remembered my friend Genevieve had told me a dream she had of me four years previously. I was marrying a South African man; it was very fast but very good, and he had an adult daughter. Alister has a twenty-year-old daughter from a previous marriage.

I told Alister about the shirt and that it was a size medium. He said, "But I am a size large; I don't think it will fit." However, after we got engaged, he tried it on, and it fit perfectly!

Over the past few years, when my life seemed barren and I was living in the "hope deferred makes the heart sick" part of Proverbs 13:12, I felt God say again and again, "Even when you can't see it, I am moving." I knew He was good, so I was just waiting to see His goodness manifest. I knew it would come.

God has also spoken to me through Ephesians 3:20—He is able to do immeasurably more than we can ask or imagine, and meeting and marrying Alister has been that for me.

And about the open door. I got married aged forty-four. The fourth letter of the Hebrew alphabet is dalet—which is pictorially an open door. Forty-four is two open doors. God opened the door for marriage at exactly the right time.

In November of 2022, Jemimah released her first novel, "Isabella's Voyage, Dare She Heed Hope's Call?" and it is fantastic! "Isabella's Voyage" is an unforgettable love story set in 1880s England and Hawaii. If you like historical fiction written in the style of Jane Austen's "Pride and Prejudice," you will love "Isabella's Voyage." I hope to see it on the big screen one day; it's that good!

21

Stacy's Story

So I will restore to you the years that the swarming locust has eaten, The crawling locust, The consuming locust, And the chewing locust...You shall eat in plenty and be satisfied, And praise the name of the Lord your God, Who has dealt wondrously with you; And My people shall never be put to shame.

Joel 2:25–26

This next story is from another dear friend, Stacy Hord Hulm.

We met after she was a guest on *The 700 Club* talking about her amazing book *A New Vision for Dating*. We were the same age, single, and believing God for our husbands. We became fast friends and prayer partners. I'll never forget the day I got a text from Stacy with her and Nick holding a marriage license! Her long wait was over! She made it to the altar about a year before I did, but I was so happy for her. I know her story of waiting and never giving up will bless you as it did me.

The Wait

One day, as I was leaving an outdoor birthday gathering near my home in Missouri, I passed a man arriving late to the party. I didn't know him personally, and I barely saw his face, but I remember thinking to myself, *I think that is Nick, who is dating one of the women at the party.* We walked past each other without a word, and I did not give it a second thought.

I was single at the time and had been for almost a decade. My journey had been one of pain, regret, grace, and restoration. After my divorce, I wish I could say I took the shorter path to restoration by running straight to God and giving Him my singleness. I certainly had been taught that in my church upbringing. But instead, I did what many who think the answer to heartache is to find a new love do—I hit the bar scene.

For a year and a half, I spent nearly every weekend partying, neglecting my children, and, quite honestly, making a fool of myself. Godly friends attempted to steer me back to God, but the notion of finding romance consumed my thoughts, and I was meeting lots of men in the hot spots every weekend.

Though I persisted in finding relationships, I couldn't keep a boyfriend to save my life! I tried, and I tried, but inevitably, the thrilling sparks of a new love would eventually fizzle out. I felt like a failure and became depressed. Other areas of my life began to fail. I drank to dull the pain that not only was my life a wreck, but my son's lives were being robbed by my deterioration.

One Friday night, I experienced something like what the

prodigal son must have experienced when, as the Bible says, "he came to himself." I was at a restaurant with my party friends when I noticed that people at other tables were gazing at us. An awareness hit me that our table, full of drinking, loud obscenities, and lewdness, was ruining the evening for families who were there to enjoy a pleasant dinner. It felt filthy, like spiritual pig-slop. Was this what I had become?

Later that night, at 2 a.m., on the drive home, I knew in my heart I wanted to run back to God, where I belonged. I wanted to be clean again, but I didn't know how to get there. A voice in my heart whispered, "Say the name of Jesus."

I hadn't prayed in months. Sin had bound me up and gagged my mouth, making me not want to pray. But I knew the name of Jesus was powerful, so I opened my mouth, and for the first time in a year and a half, I whispered, "Jesus." I whispered it again, "Jesus." Then something in my soul broke loose, and I began shouting it, "Jesus!" I got home and cried myself to sleep.

Two nights later, a friend told me how on Friday night, at 2 a.m., she was in bed asleep when God woke her up and told her she needed to pray for me. Then I put it together: As I was driving home shouting "Jesus," God woke this precious woman up to pray for me. He heard me.

God saved me from certain self-destruction. What had appeared as new-found freedom in the party crowd was, in fact, a form of slavery in which the yoke tightened day by day, choking the life out of me. When God broke the yoke, I lost all desire to follow that life anymore or date those kinds of men. I deleted and blocked numbers and closed that door.

Months of godly sorrow followed. I spent a great deal of time crying and repenting. The more I repented with tears, the more God comforted me, and in a new twist, this headstrong girl who had been set on finding a man to marry asked God what *His* will was. His answer was to "wait." I thought I heard "for six months," but it would be seven years before I would date again.

For seven years I did not so much as have a coffee date. I enjoyed God and my boys to the fullest. God filled our house with joy, unity, and laughter. During those years, God gave me a greater sense of being *in the moment* with my sons. I still remember those moments with fantastic detail. I was more alive than I had ever been.

I still silently yearned for marriage "someday," but as I wrestled with a damaged past, I wasn't sure I deserved another chance. I decided to fast and seek God. While praying one afternoon, I was stunned to suddenly see an open vision. In front of me was a dark-haired man sitting in baseball stands. I did not know him, and he was not the type of guy I would naturally be drawn to. In addition, I was struck with a knowledge that I would not initially *like* this man. Puzzled, I asked God, "You're going to give me a man I don't like?" I was disappointed. I had always chased after the fireworks and thrills of new romance, and this sounded, well, boring. But I submitted, "Have Your way, Lord."

There were many things about the vision I did not understand, so I wrote it down, trusting that God would give me the interpretation soon. The baseball stands stood out to me. "My sons play baseball.

Certainly, I will meet him at a game," I mused. "Maybe he has a son that plays baseball too. That would be perfect—we love sports!"

At the games my eyes scanned the crowds at perchance meeting him. Unconsciously, I was trying to fulfill the vision myself instead of "leaning *not* unto my own understanding," as Proverbs 3:5 tells us.

A month later, I was standing in church chatting with some women about my desire to remarry. My friend said, "I see Stacy with a man who has dark hair and..." I didn't hear the last words because, at that very moment, the same vision popped in front of me again! I was beyond words knowing full well what that second vision meant. When God gives us a word, He establishes it by two witnesses. It is confirmation that *He* is going to do it. However, it does not necessarily mean that it will come to pass immediately. In many circumstances, it is meant to sustain us and encourage us while we wait for what could be many years for that word to manifest.

Another year went by. And another. I studied the Bible for hours a day and walked with God. I wrote my book *A New Vision for Dating*, which landed me a spot as a guest on *The 700 Club*, and I entered an exciting time of TV and radio appearances, speaking at conferences and ministering to singles. Then, my sons graduated and left for college, leaving me an empty nester.

During this time, Wendy and I struck up a friendship and became prayer partners. We called each other often and prayed for long hours over our dating lives. I felt that my husband was coming soon. After all, I had finished raising my sons and refrained from dating for those seven years. Surely God was going to reward that.

But another year passed, and I was getting slightly resentful that the vision hadn't been fulfilled yet. Then the dam broke when, one afternoon, my date for the evening canceled. Disheartened, I broke into tears. I cried, "Where are You, God? I thought You had someone for me. Did I hear You wrong?" As tears flowed, I had a sudden remembrance of the vision of the man sitting in the baseball stands. Then God spoke, "In the same way you loved sitting in the stands, watching your sons play baseball, you will love being married to this man."

By that one sentence, my heart turned from grief to hope. Only God knew how much I loved watching my boys play ball. I had butterflies in my stomach on game days. I felt pure joy watching my boys run, play, and hit home runs against beautiful sunset nights. When they grew up and left home, those memories pained me; I missed them so much. All this time, I mistakenly thought the baseball stands represented *how* I would meet my husband, but instead, they represented the *joy* I would have when I married him. "You will love being married to this man." I would have those butterflies again. My empty nest would be replaced with laughter, sunsets, and excitement, and I would love it all! That's exactly what I had been praying for! I felt rejuvenated.

Wendy and I continued to pray. She traveled to Missouri to stay with me during the New Year's holidays, and we spent the time praying for our future husbands. A decade earlier, I would have been out partying, looking for a man, but now, Wendy and I were in my small apartment, praying for one.

More years passed, life brought changes and grandchildren, and though I kept praying, I had almost given up. In fact, I was entertaining the idea of becoming a missionary in Indonesia to minister to single women. However, one day, my daughter-in-law thought it would be a great idea for me to try an online dating site. I disagreed. Somewhere along the line, I had adopted the belief that online dating wasn't of God. I believed in the old-fashioned way of meeting at church, preferably in a Bible study group, and having a divine connection on "holy ground." But she persisted, and I was online for four whole days. And alas, that is how I met Nick.

We only spoke through messages and hadn't met yet, when my sister suddenly died, and I had to fly to Oregon to decide for the burial and sale of her house. I was under an enormous amount of stress and grief. Nick checked in on me every day, and that impressed me. I started envisioning the possibilities.

When I returned from Oregon, we decided to meet. I thought, *This might be it! I will see him, and my long search will be over!* But that did not happen. During our meeting, the communication between us was dry. We did not mesh, and I just could not see myself with him. Discouraged, I drove home, not sure I would ever speak to him again.

But he kept calling, and as weeks went by, my opinion of Nick changed. He was refreshingly genuine and authentic, and he had an adorable way of smiling when he teased me. I discovered that underneath his manly hunting and fishing exterior, he was quite soft-hearted and thoughtful.

I had a reoccurring thought that I knew him from somewhere. Then I realized he was the guy I had seen at the birthday party four years earlier. He was *that* Nick! Though I hardly noticed him that day, he had noticed *me,* and God planted a little seed. So when he saw me on the dating app, he jumped at the chance to talk to me. God was working even when I didn't know it.

Lest you think it was all cupids and rainbows after that, the truth is, we still had disagreements, and I still wasn't convinced he checked all the boxes. I broke up with him several times because I did not have all the answers and my feelings were wishy-washy. However, I could not deny that in the vision, I had the same unsettled feelings and reaction.

People so often rely only on immediate fireworks and attraction to decide on a mate, and although that can happen, it often leads us down a wrong path. God, being as brilliant as He is, has a much better idea— to grow, by His own hand, a true, genuine, and lasting attraction, not the counterfeits like I had pursued before. Zechariah 4:10 says to not despise God's small beginnings. His way is often to start with a seed and grow it into something beautiful with deep roots.

Though God had given me the vision, I still had to step out in faith to accept it. Gradually, He lifted the veil, and I discovered what an absolute treasure Nick is. God had not been hiding him *from* me; He had been hiding him *for* me! I had never in my life respected a man like I did Nick, and my smoldering sticks of interest in him grew into a full-blown fire for him. I was in love, and it was thrilling!

After eight months, we were married in a sweet and simple

backyard wedding. The beautiful conclusion of fourteen years of singleness and waiting. God was at that altar with us. He saw the vision to its fulfillment. He is good for His word.

During the nuptials, Nick's voice broke, and tears ran down his face, an image I will always treasure. It wasn't just my journey that had taken years; his did as well. On the day we passed each other at the birthday party, he, too, was searching. We were within feet of each other that day, but it simply was not time yet.

We've been married for nearly five years now, and we laugh almost daily. I absolutely love being with him, and our life is filled with numerous adventures. Sometimes I'll be at work and think of him, and I get butterflies in my stomach. My youth has been restored.

"He forgives all my sins and heals all my diseases. He redeems me from death and crowns me with love and tender mercies. He fills my life with good things. My youth is renewed like the eagle's" (Psalm 103:5).

In January 2021, Nick and I joined Wendy and her husband, Bill, at Snowshoe Mountain Ski Resort in West Virginia for the New Year's holidays—exactly seven years after Wendy and I spent a weekend praying for our future spouses. Were our prayers seven years earlier the reason we had husbands? I believe so. God hears our prayers. He heard me when I was a drunk party girl who needed delivering; He heard me when I wanted a restored relationship with my sons, and He heard me when I was a lonely woman wanting to marry. He hears.

Not long ago, Nick and I were talking about prayer and how God rewards us when we place our faith in Him. Nick said, "I'm your reward for all those years you waited, right?" I replied, "You sure are, babe!"

22

Cheri's Story

*"You shall no more be termed Forsaken, and your land
shall no more be termed Desolate, but you shall be called
My Delight is in Her, and your land Married; for the Lord
delights in you, and your land shall be married."*

Isaiah 62:4 (ESV)

I was that girl. Curly hair, glasses, bad skin, shy, wore homemade
clothes, and to top it off, my dad was a Pentecostal pastor! There were
so many reasons to be left out, pushed to the side, and forgotten about.
But I was nice and fairly smart, so I did have some good friends! But
not boyfriends. The only guys interested in me were the ones who
were a lot like me—unattractive and left out! So in my early twenties,
I started working at a bank and then had money to start dressing
like the other girls. And I had started wearing contacts. Things were
looking up! Or so I thought.

When I was about thirteen, the Lord made a promise to me
that one day I would be married, and my husband and I would be in

ministry together. So after that, every guy that came along who sang, preached, or was a pastor's son became a potential mate in my eyes. But those guys were not interested in me, which led to making poor decisions in dating due to my insecurity and fear of not being loved.

At one point, I even signed up for eharmony only to get "matched" with men I would never consider dating! It seemed everyone was trying to set me up with some friend, relative, neighbor, etc. And I did go out with a few of those guys only to be disappointed and sometimes even embarrassed.

The loneliness was so intense. I was always the third or fifth wheel on outings. The night would ultimately end with me curled up in bed crying and asking God, "Why does this have to be my life?" It was hard to go to bridal showers, weddings, baby showers, etc. I wanted to be a bride! I couldn't seem to control my disappointment and jealousy.

By the time I was thirty, I was over it. I decided to move away from home and see if that helped. Surely part of the problem was that I lived in a small town! So off to Nashville I went. It wasn't long before I had a job as an administrative assistant at a major Christian record label. I lived there for about three and a half years, and it was a wonderful time. I had a great group of friends—almost every one of them was single too. My life was very full, and I did go out on a few dates, but still, nothing lasting.

The truth is I was having so much fun that being single wasn't as much of an issue. Very rarely did anyone in Nashville ask me if I was married or dating. That was such a huge relief! However, every single time I went home to Florida for a visit, several people would ask if I had "met anyone special." It was exhausting. So much so that one Sunday, as soon as my dad (the pastor) started the altar call, I slipped out of church to avoid the inevitable questions about my singlehood. Well, wouldn't you know that one little elderly lady saw me get up and met me in the lobby—only to ask me that dreaded question! Ugh! I just couldn't avoid it.

Finally, being away from my family got the best of me, and I moved back home. This time around, I went on a few dates, but still, nothing was working out or felt right. The only thing that brought me joy and fulfillment was being an aunt. My brother, my only sibling, had three children, and they were (and still are) the light of my life! About two years after returning home, our family faced a terrible tragedy. My oldest nephew took his life at the age of seventeen. There are no words to describe the pain of his death. I was the one to stay strong for my parents and my brother and his family. About a year later, I began to have panic attacks. They were horrible. I couldn't drive very far without having to pull to the side of the road and call my dad to come get me. I finally ended up on low-dose anxiety medication. This was *not* the way I wanted to live my life. Finally, after much prayer and some counseling, God beautifully healed me! It was at that time that I received a call from a church in Central Florida concerning a job opportunity. And once again, I moved away from home to try to start a new life.

This began the whole cycle again. People trying to set me up, and guys asking me out—but they were not the ones I wanted to say yes to! Then, I fell into a wrong relationship that took up way too much of my time, mental energy, and relationship with God. Desperation is an ugly monster. I tried to force God to do things *my* way. After all, I had been trying *His* way, and it just wasn't working. But once again, I was dumped. And this time, it felt like complete failure. My heart was broken more than ever before. This time, as I turned to the Lord, He began to tug at my heart about moving back home.

In November of 2010, my mother had surgery, and I went home to take care of her. A friend was getting married during my stay, and I had made plans to attend. Just a few days before the wedding, my best friend sent me a text telling me all about this new guy at her church—the same church where the wedding would be held. She told me he was very good-looking, was a surfer, was divorced, and was about nine years younger than me. By this time, I was forty-eight years old, and a younger man sounded intriguing.

I had forgotten about her text by the time the date of the wedding rolled around. However, as I walked up the church steps, I saw the most gorgeous man standing in the lobby—in a tuxedo! My heart did a flip-flop! My friend confirmed that this was the guy she had told me about. Unbeknownst to me, the pastor had been talking to this guy about me! We didn't actually meet until the next night while at church. He had noticed me at the wedding as well and was quick to introduce himself. His name was Ben.

Ben and I began to talk and eventually exchanged phone numbers. We were able to see each other some while I was staying with my mom. I went back to Lakeland for a few weeks, then came home for Christmas. It was at that time that I told my family that I was ready to move back, but it would be in the spring. However, I was offered a free moving truck if I could make the move in mid-January. So I did! And guess who came and helped me move? Ben and the pastor!

Ben and I began dating. He had a call on his life to be in ministry, and he had been spending a lot of time being mentored by his pastor. I began to become more and more confident that he was the one for me, but there was an issue. He came from a divorced family and did not want that to be his story. His ex-wife was not a Christian, and that issue was the main cause of their divorce. He was still believing God for her salvation and the restoration of their marriage. So we broke up. For the first time in my life, I was able to have peace about the breakup. I couldn't play second fiddle to another woman, so I knew that if Ben was God's plan for me, then God would have to work it out. A scripture that the Lord had given me years ago was Isaiah 62:4, "*You shall* no longer *be* termed Forsaken, Nor *shall your land* any more *be* termed Desolate; But *you shall be* called Hephzibah, *and your land* Beulah; For the Lord delights in *you, And your land shall be married.*" This verse gave me the strength to walk in peace!

In August of 2011, we went to dinner as friends. Ben kissed me, and I asked him what that was all about! He said he had been praying, and he realized that I was the woman he wanted to be with. So now we began dating again—this time seriously. However, we never discussed marriage...

A Walk on the Beach...

June 2nd, 2012, was my fiftieth birthday. We spent the day together and ended up at the home of friends on Pensacola Beach. I had asked for a walk on the beach at sunset—something we had never done, even though he is a surfer! Well, in the middle of the afternoon—not at sunset—he said he wanted us to go for that walk. He even went and changed clothes! What? As we walked onto the beach, there were two weddings taking place—one to the right of us and one to the left of us. How awkward! Then, he asked if I had ever considered a beach wedding. To which I replied, "Every girl that has grown up close to the water has dreamed of a beach wedding at some point!" As we sunk our toes in the famous white sand of Pensacola, we decided to sit down in front of a beach house that his dad had helped to build many years ago. As we sat there, Ben began to tell me how much he loved me and that he knew that I was God's gift to him. We hugged, and then something felt weird with one of his arms—he was reaching into his pocket! Suddenly, I began to shake! Oh my word! It's happening! Ben proposed to me, right there on the sand, and gave me the most beautiful engagement ring! Then he took me in his arms and began to pray over us! What a moment! What a birthday gift!

The joy of calling friends and family and spreading the news was tremendous! And, of course, the obligatory Facebook posts. Now we were on our way to planning a wedding and our life together. Doors for ministry opportunities also opened up as we truly saw God's hand at work in our lives.

We were married on November 3, 2012. It was a picture-perfect beach wedding with friends and family. Our vows were tailor-made; we picked just the right songs, and we had four pastors praying over us.

A few years later, my husband gave surf lessons to a lady named Rhonda and her son from Louisiana. Rhonda's husband was a pastor, and we all met and became friends. About a year or so after that, I got a phone call from Rhonda. She told me all about her friend Wendy Griffith of *The 700 Club*, who was in her early fifties and still single. She had shared our story with Wendy, and she wanted to meet us! The next thing I knew, Wendy and Rhonda were in my living room during a home Bible study that I was leading at the time! And I had the privilege of praying with Wendy for her dream of being married! A subsequent visit brought Wendy back with TV cameras and a film crew to capture my love story with Ben. You see, the other part of the story is that Ben had not been raised in a Christian home. He had lived a life of crime, drugs, and alcohol until he met Jesus on the side of the road after an automobile accident. Thanks to Wendy and *The 700 Club*, both of our stories have now gone around the world and reached thousands of people with a message of hope, grace, love, and promises fulfilled!

It seemed like it took God a *really* long time to bring His promise to pass in my life. But those many years of waiting have faded away as we have now celebrated our tenth anniversary. God has been so faithful! And if I had married sooner, I would have never had the opportunity to minister to so many women with words of hope and encouragement. God's timing does have purpose!

You Didn't Miss It!

If you'd like to see Cheri and Ben's amazing love story that aired on CBN, just Google "True Love Waits: Surfer Couple Lives Out God's Promises/CBN."

23

It's Not Too Late

*"Delight yourself in the Lord, and He will give you
the desires of your heart."*

Psalm 37:4

Life Beings At...

You know that famous saying, "Life begins at forty"? Well, that was true for me in a lot of ways. My career skyrocketed when I hit forty, and I was living my dream as an international correspondent for CBN News. My passport was well stamped with exotic destinations from Israel to New Zealand to the Philippines, and the stories themselves took me on many exciting adventures—some even a little dangerous, which made it even more fun in my opinion. I loved the adrenaline rush and the challenge of pursuing a story, writing it, having my editor match the voice track with just the right video or pictures, and getting it on the air by show time—for me, there was nothing more fulfilling, but that, of course, was just one part of my life. The other part of my life—my personal life was decidedly "on the shelf," a rather dusty shelf, and was the opposite of exciting and adventurous. I can remember entire years passing without a single date (hard to admit that one)! To be honest, I was so busy and having so much fun with work and travel that I almost didn't care—well, except for that huge meltdown I had when I turned forty and screamed in my car at the top of my lungs because I was still single. But somehow, work filled that space, and I was, for the most part, content to wait—I mean, what choice did I really have anyway?

As I entered my late forties with an ex-boyfriend, a shattered heart, and no prospects on the horizon, it felt like I was back at ground zero—waiting again...but now, more than anything, waiting for my heart to heal. I couldn't date. As much as I wanted to, as much as my family and friends told me to "get back out there," I just couldn't. I wasn't ready. The other guy still had my heart, and it was going to take some work to get it back. When I look back at photos of myself from that time, I just want to hug that person—there was so much pain and hurt in my eyes. I honestly hate to even remember how I felt back then. The only thing I miss about that time is how thin I was. I could eat a pint of Ben & Jerry's every night (Chunky Monkey was my flavor of choice) and not gain a pound. Who knew that heartbreak could burn so many calories!

Mourn and Move On

God told me to mourn and move on—so why was the "moving on" part taking so long? I remember finding out my ex-boyfriend was back online dating within a week of our breakup! No doubt trying to find a quick fix to the emptiness a breakup causes, no matter who does the breaking up. As much as I wanted to fill my aching heart with a new relationship, that was not going to happen for me. God was doing a deep work, and the healing process would not be rushed. The good news is the season of mourning did end—finally, and almost without warning, I had feelings for another guy! This was still a couple of years before I met Bill, yet I remember how amazing it felt to have romantic feelings for someone again! It felt like my heart was thawing from years of a bitter, cold winter—I felt alive; I felt excited and, most of all, happy that I was now officially ready to move on. This new "relationship," or whatever it was, was mostly long-distance texting and phone calls with one amazing date in the Southern California hills that seemed like it was right out of a movie—and although it was short-lived and he wasn't the one, I will always be grateful for how God used this person to restart my heart. I was ready to love again.

Give Me Another Mountain

I know the slogan is "Life begins at forty"—but for me, life (at least my personal life) was getting a lot more interesting in my fifties. I started my fifth decade by summiting the world's largest free-standing mountain—Kilimanjaro. But the high mountains kept calling, and at fifty-two, I summited Everest Base Camp in Nepal (17,598 ft.), but in order to get an even better view of the world's highest peak, we climbed an additional 1,000 feet to a place called Kala Patthar

(18,519 ft.), known for its up-close and unobstructed views of Mount Everest (29,031 ft.). Truly worth the extra effort. I loved the Nepalese people, and one of our Sherpa guides on the trek, fifty-two-year-old Kami Rita Sherpa, has held the world record since 2018 for the most ascents to the summit of Mount Everest. As of May 7, 2002, he broke his own record when he scaled the world's tallest mountain for the twenty-sixth time. I'm happy to call him a friend.

Although I was still single and wanting to meet someone, God was taking His time bringing anyone of interest into my life. So I would say to God, "You're obviously not ready to bring my husband yet, or even a boyfriend, so please give me another mountain to climb!" And God would oblige me. I've always loved the physical and mental challenge of climbing, seeing new and exotic places, and the thrill of making it to the top with God's help.

As you'll recall from chapter one, it was on the Inca Trail to Machu Picchu in 2017 that I asked my friend Ginna to fix me up with someone when we got back home. So in many ways, you could say the mountains led me to my husband. I literally burst into tears when I wrote that last line, "the mountains led me to my husband." There's something I can't explain about my love for the mountains— is it because I'm from West Virginia, the mountain state as it's called? Or those countless climbs up my beloved Old Rag here in Virginia where I would talk to God, pray, and pour out my heart to Him? I don't know, but I do know that God was with me on every mountain adventure, and He heard every prayer and caught every tear. God hears your prayers, too, and perhaps the lesson in all this is—do what you love while you wait. Maybe for you, it's biking or cooking or salsa dancing or jumping out of airplanes! (I have friends who do this, but it's definitely not my thing.) Whatever it is, don't stop living and celebrating life now while you wait. That thing that makes you you, that makes you come alive, that makes you happy may be the very thing that leads you to your future husband or wife; it did for me— even though it was indirectly through a hiking friend who knew Bill.

Enjoy the life God has given you now. Don't wait. Have faith. If you do these things, I believe your biggest adventures, your biggest joys, and your biggest loves are still ahead. You didn't miss it.

24

You Still Deserve the Fairy Tale

"Fear not, for I have redeemed you;
I have called you by your name; you are mine."

Isaiah 43:1

I was having lunch with a longtime friend from CBN recently who is not only beautiful and sweet but seems to have the picture-perfect family. Her husband is movie-star handsome and loves the Lord, and together they have three beautiful daughters.

As we reminisced and caught up, she shared something from her past that gave me chills. Sharon (we'll call her) grew up in the church, loved Jesus, and was definitely going to wait until marriage to have sex for the first time. From an early age, she had a heart for missions, and when she was eighteen, she packed her bags and moved to Hawaii to be a part of a popular ministry. She loved working with overseas missions and seeing people from all over the world come to know Jesus.

One day she met a boy who was going to college on the same island (he was not a part of the ministry she was involved in).

Sharon told me what had happened.

"This relationship was very unhealthy for the woman of God that I knew I was called to be. He was not a Christian, and right away I knew this was not right for me. However, the temptation was easier to give in to since he didn't have a conviction regarding intimacy before marriage. It started out innocently enough. I was attending a sports event hosted by his college, and he casually walked up to me and started a conversation. He was charming and funny, and we chatted with ease. Being young and unaware that more could happen never entered my mind, so the temptation was not obvious right away. It was a perfect scenario of comfort and ease that set me up for sexual sin," Sharon said.

"So I now felt like I was living a double life, and of course, I knew better, but there was a part of me that wanted to see what life was like on the 'other side.' This was the first time as a young woman I felt the strong effects of sin and how easy it can be to feel stuck in sin and shame all at the same time," she said.

Jesus Paid the Price

"At the end of the relationship, I walked away knowing I had made my sin bigger than what Jesus died for. I was walking in guilt that my life, especially 'marriage,' would no longer be blessed because of my sexual sin," Sharon remembered.

You Still Deserve the Fairy Tale

Devasted and heartbroken, Sharon called her mother back in Virginia, who she'd always been close with, to confess. She told her mother, "I gave away the one thing I was saving and was always told to protect as a child of God." Sharon knew there was a chance her mom could come back with a comment that could make her feel worse than she already did. However, her mother listened to her story and then, without hesitating, said, "You still deserve the fairy tale..."

I got a million chill bumps when Sharon recounted those life-giving words of hope.

Sharon told me...

"It felt like a waterfall of love being poured over my broken heart. It was so unexpected because the enemy had been telling me so many lies that were the exact opposite of what my mother said to me. The enemy is so good at making God's children feel stuck in shame that we don't keep moving forward into all God has for us. So my mom's words took me back to what I always knew about Jesus and His love for me. The cross that Jesus died on took the sin and shame I was feeling because they were never meant for me to hold onto or go back and try to pick back up at any point," she said.

She Didn't Miss It

"The recording in my mind that was playing 'You messed up, and now you missed it' was replaced with 'You still deserve the fairy tale.' These five words have allowed me to go toward all God has for me. His promises are so good and alive in my life today. I married a man who loves Jesus and me with his whole heart, and we have three daughters who are our greatest joys. Now our family is in ministry together, and the dreams that the enemy tried to steal are being walked over by God's incredible love and grace," Sharon told me.

Sharon's mom had the heart of Jesus and spoke the exact words that Sharon needed to hear at exactly the right time. Maybe you feel you have "messed up" and therefore disqualified yourself from God's best—I'm here to tell you that you've been believing a lie. Just like Sharon, you still deserve the fairy tale. God still has plan A for you. Forgive yourself and dust yourself off because Jesus has already forgiven you. First John 1:9 says, "*If we confess our sins, He is faithful and just to forgive us our sins and to cleanse us from all unrighteousness.*"

The Bible says the power of life and death are in the tongue, and Sharon's story brought much-needed healing and life to a lady who had waited decades to hear that Jesus had paid the price for her sin.

"I shared this story at a women's Bible study, and an eighty-year-old woman came up to me and said, 'I wish my mom would have told me that when I was young.' She said her life would have looked so different. This made me very aware of the lies the enemy keeps us believing for far too long. Jesus died a brutal death so that we could have freedom from sin," Sharon added.

"One thing that helped me renew my mind when the enemy's lies would try to tell me the opposite of God's Word was to read His promises to me daily. Staying in the Bible reminded me of God's promises over my life more than the enemy's threats," Sharon said. "Two verses that are close to my heart are..."

"It is for freedom that Christ has set us free. Stand firm, then, and do not let yourselves be burdened again by a yoke of slavery" (Galatians 5:1, NIV).

> *Praise be to the God and Father of our Lord Jesus Christ! In his great mercy he has given us new birth into a living hope through the resurrection of Jesus Christ from the dead, and into an inheritance that can never perish, spoil or fade. This inheritance is kept in heaven for you, who through faith are shielded by God's power until the coming of the salvation that is ready to be revealed in the last time.*
>
> 1 Peter 1:3–5 (NIV)

The Power of the Cross

"It's so easy to discredit the power of the cross in the moments that we feel we aren't worthy of His forgiveness. If you are holding onto your shame more than Jesus, it's time to let it go into the Healer's hands. He can heal your heart and mind because He knows you better than anyone ever will. You are called by God, and He wants all the good that you inherited as His child to be yours until you see Him face to face for all eternity. You are the King's daughter or son, and no sin or shame can replace that," Sharon said.

You still deserve the fairy tale. You didn't miss it.

25

Lessons from Kilimanjaro

"How beautiful upon the mountains are the feet of him who brings good news, Who proclaims peace, Who brings glad tidings of good things, Who proclaims salvation, Who says to Zion, 'Your God reigns!'"

Isaiah 52:7

As you know by now, I love the mountains. I can't remember a time when I didn't love scaling mountains—just for the sheer joy of climbing and that feeling of accomplishment when you reach the top! But a few years ago, I felt the need—actually, it was a burning desire of my heart—to climb a really high mountain! And that mountain was Kilimanjaro—the tallest free-standing mountain in the world! Nineteen thousand three hundred forty-one feet to be exact.

The only problem with my dream to climb Mount Kilimanjaro was—my boss wouldn't let me go. It was the summer of 2013, and I had just landed my dream job as a *700 Club* co-host. Unfortunately, about that same time, former NBC news anchor Anne Curry had to be famously rescued off Kilimanjaro. My boss simply said, "I don't want you to go; it's too dangerous—people die." I was disappointed but understood and didn't want to upset my boss, so I put the dream back on the shelf.

A year later—the desire came back stronger than ever! I was turning fifty, and I wanted to do something epic for my birthday! I remember being in my dressing room crying because I wanted to go so badly but was afraid to ask my boss again. I heard the Lord say, "Fear Me!" In other words, stop being afraid and just ask again.

So I got up the nerve and knocked on his door. When he answered and invited me in—I burst into tears! I'm sure he thought something terrible had happened, and he was obviously concerned. "What's the matter?" he asked. I answered through tears, "I still want to climb Kilimanjaro!" "Okay, calm down. Why do you want to climb Kilimanjaro?" he asked. "Because I need a bigger mountain!" (That was really the best excuse I had, but it was from the heart!) I explained to him that I'd climbed this one mountain in Virginia—Old Rag—more than fifty times, maybe closer to seventy times now, and even though I loved it, I needed a new and bigger challenge. The Bible says the king's heart is in the hand of the Lord (Proverbs 21:1), and that day, God changed my boss's heart, and he gave me his blessing. Sometimes it doesn't hurt to shed a few tears as well.

What would you do if fear was not a factor?

So I booked my trip and bought my plane ticket to Tanzania. And then, out of the blue, my boss's words came back to haunt me. "People die on that mountain—altitude sickness can kill you." Suddenly, fear gripped my heart! I was sitting in my car thinking, *What am I doing? What if I can't handle the altitude?* Did I have what it took to make it to the top? I'd never been that high. The highest I'd ever climbed was about 12,000 feet in Colorado, and I currently lived at sea level! Kilimanjaro stands over nineteen thousand feet high. I prayed—God help me! At the very moment I was having those panicky thoughts, I turned on K-LOVE Christian radio to hear the lady DJ say:

"What would you do if fear was not a factor?" Peace flooded my heart; I had my answer. I knew what I would do—I would climb Mount Kilimanjaro.

Preparing to Go!

I only had a month to prepare physically—I know most people train for six months to a year or more, but this is how I roll, and living at sea level, the only way to really train for high altitude is to increase your cardio—so I got a personal trainer, a friend of mine from church, and we would run the one and only hill in Virginia Beach called Mount Trashmore. When I got to the top, I would do push-ups while still breathless to hopefully simulate low oxygen and prepare my lungs for high altitude.

God Loves Mountains

I'm always amazed at how many times mountains are mentioned in the Bible; at least fifty-eight scriptures mention them. So I have to think God loves mountains too. As I was preparing physically, I was also preparing spiritually. I asked the Lord for a scripture, and it became very dear to me before, during, and after the climb:

"You who bring good news to Zion, Go up on a High Mountain! You who bring good news to Jerusalem, lift up your voice with a shout, lift it up, Do not be afraid; say to the towns of Judah, 'Here is your God!'" (Isaiah 40:9, NIV).

My favorite version is in the Message:

> *Climb a High Mountain, Zion. [Wendy] You're the preacher of good news! Speak loud and clear. Don't be timid! Tell the cities of Judah, "Look! Your God!" Look at him! GOD, the Master, comes in power, ready to go into action. He is going to pay back his enemies and reward those who have loved him.*

I love that the Message version is almost a mandate, a command—climb a high mountain! Not a short mountain, mind you—but a high mountain. For some reason every time I read that scripture, it brings tears to my eyes. I knew I was supposed to go.

What I didn't know is that I would be tested in every way you can be tested. But I took off for Africa full of faith—and thankfully wearing my brand new hiking boots because my bags did not arrive when I landed in Africa (my first test). Thankfully, before we left the hotel for the mountain several days later, one of my bags with my sleeping bag, backpack, trekking poles, and an extra rain jacket did arrive—but my suitcase with all my cool new clothes, glacier sunglasses, warm hats, my big new red down jacket did not! For my first three days on Kilimanjaro, I wore exactly what I had worn on the airplane four days prior—the same pants, shirt, undies (which I washed), socks, and again, thank God I wore my boots on the plane (your most important piece of equipment). I had to borrow and rent winter clothing for the higher elevations in case my other bag did not arrive while I was on the mountain. Our climb started in the rainforest at about 6,000 feet above sea level, and fortunately it wasn't that cold yet. From the trail we could see coffee farms and hear the monkeys howling from the trees. It looked a lot like *Jurassic Park*—lush, green, and tropical.

On day three, miraculously, my bag arrived! My neon lime green Samsonite suitcase (how they lost that I'll never know) was carried up by the porters—it was like Christmas on the mountain! I was so thankful because the weather was turning much colder.

Migraine on the Mountain

Unfortunately, that same day around 14,000 feet, I developed a terrible migraine—one of the worst I'd ever had. I threw up for two days and got separated from my group because I was hiking so slowly—and it was hailing! Tiny pea-sized hail that stung when it hit your cheeks. I was used to migraines and wasn't going to let this stop me, but my emotional state that day was not good. Fortunately, my Tanzanian guide, Moody, stayed with me and even held my hair back for me when I had to throw up. I heard the Holy Spirit whisper, "This will be your hardest day," and it was.

Psalm 121

I remember that day stopping to take a photo of the now emerging snow-covered peak of Kilimanjaro and quoting Psalm 121, *"I will lift up my eyes to the Hills, from whence comes my help? My help comes from the Lord, the Maker of Heaven and Earth."* I knew as hard as the climb had been so far—God was with me and would help me.

Cold Nights

The other big challenge (test) was the cold nights in the tent—no matter how much I bundled up, I could not get warm. I even had the cooks put boiling water in my water bottles so I could put those in my sleeping bag at night. It helped some, but I still froze and was always thankful for daylight. My tent mate's name was Mary—a nurse from New York who I was paired with for the journey. She had a mouth like a sailor but was a good person and a good tent mate—we prayed together a few times and helped each other when the other was sick.

Summit Night

Finally, Summit night arrived. It was our fifth night on the mountain. My fellow hikers (all thirteen of us) took off at midnight with our headlamps, heavy parkas, and gloves and headed up the mountain in a single-file line. It was cold—below freezing. We were already about 16,000 feet high! At that elevation every step is hard; your breathing is labored, and you walk at turtle pace. In Swahili they say *pole, pole*—which means slowly—and that's the only way to make it to the top of Kilimanjaro....*slowly.*

Do Not Fear—Finish!

Several hours into the night hike—it must have been around 5 a.m., but it was still pitch black despite a full moon—I began to see a few people coming down the mountain with oxygen masks! These were young people, otherwise healthy-looking people! And they were frantically being carried by porters or guides down the mountain. I couldn't help but wonder, *Will that be me in a few minutes?* Fear gripped my heart—the kind of fear that paralyzes you—I literally felt like I couldn't move. I prayed, "Lord, what should I do?" I heard the still, small voice of the Holy Spirit, and He simply said, "Do not fear—finish!"

Still, I was afraid. I didn't want to be carried down the mountain or worse. I looked at my guide, Moody, and uttered the words I thought I would never say, "I'm scared; I want to go down." But with a very calm voice and words I believe came straight from heaven, he looked at me and said:

"Wendy, this is the place most people turn around."

When Moody said, "This is the place most people turn around!" Something ignited in my spirit—a deep knowing that I had to finish! Turning back was no longer an option. I didn't want to be one of the people who gave up, even though, at that point, I had no idea how far we were from the summit. It was still dark; I was exhausted; my nose was running—and I was afraid! But I knew I didn't want to be in the company of those who "turned back." I love how God knew exactly what I needed to hear in that moment. It infused me with the courage and strength I needed to keep going! I looked at Moody and said, "Let's finish!"

Stella Point

Just an hour or two later, the sun came up; my energy returned, and we reached the first summit called Stella Point—which stands at a lofty 18,888 feet. I gave Moody a big hug and cried like a baby! I was so thankful I hadn't turned back! I knew we were going to make it now! We only had about 450 more feet to go to make it to the summit—Uhuru Peak, which means *freedom*! Four hundred and fifty feet may sound close, but at elevation, it still took us another hour to reach the summit! But once we reached Stella Point, it did get easier because it went from what felt like a vertical climb to a more gradual uphill climb to the top of Africa.

Somewhere between Stella Point and the summit, I ran into this sweet girl from England who had seen me days earlier when I was throwing up on the side of the trail. We hugged, and she said, "I didn't know if you'd make it!"

Finally, we reached the summit—Uhuru Peak. I took a deep breath and was surprised by how easy I was breathing—mainly because we were no longer exerting ourselves with an uphill climb. Moody and I caught up with some others from our group and quickly took photos with the big Kilimanjaro Summit sign behind us. Believe it or not, there's not much to see once you get to the top except a big glacier on the side of the mountain; we took a quick look and then hightailed it down the mountain.

Remember when I almost turned around? I was only about two hours from the summit! I didn't know how close I was!

Fear Almost Robbed Me of My Victory

Fear almost robbed me of my victory because I lost my focus. I had my eyes on the darkness, the exhaustion, and others who were not doing so well, and it almost caused me to turn back. The truth is we want it to be easy, but it's just not! You must have a mindset that you are in it to win it! You're not in it to make it halfway—*you've come too far* to turn back now. There was only one person in our group, a sixty-two-year-old woman who was hiking with her son, who appeared to be doing fine but decided, just short of the summit, to turn around. She'd had enough and didn't push on for the top—I still wonder if she wished she'd gone for it because she was so close.

Whatever mountain you're climbing right now, I believe the Lord is saying:

"Don't stop! Don't look at your circumstances or the other people who are giving up; finish what I've told you to do." When I saw the people coming down with oxygen masks, I lost my faith—all of those wonderful scriptures and promises that God had placed in my heart and all the peace I had went right out the window! But God didn't let me give up! He had the right person at the right time speak the right words to me. "This is the place most people turn back." I will never forget that moment because God used Moody to give me courage and faith to keep going. Whatever you're going through, whatever mountain you're climbing, keep your eyes on Jesus! You are closer than you think. Do you need a breakthrough in a certain area of your life? You are closer than you think! Are you praying for an answer to something that hasn't come yet? You're closer than you think! Are you waiting on God to bring you a new job, a spouse? A healing? Don't you dare give up now! Don't throw in the towel now! You are only 450 feet away from the summit! You might be just a hundred feet away! Some of you might be two feet away from your victory!

You Win!

Later, when I was back home, I asked God why. What was this epic climb to the rooftop of Africa really all about? Why did I feel the need to do this in the first place? And I heard God say, "You win!"

And then He said, "It's time to reap the spoils!"

You know the saying, "To the victor goes the spoils!" Here's how the dictionary defines "spoils":

"The spoils of victory are the extra bonuses, perks, and treasure you get for winning." In other words, it's way more than just "bragging rights"—it's the overflow of blessing. In Louisiana they have a phrase called lagniappe, pronounced *lan-yap*, which means the extra gravy or the extra blessing.

I love this story from the Bible about "spoils."

In 2 Chronicles 20:25:

When Jehoshaphat and his people came to take away their
spoil, they found among them an abundance of valuables on
the dead bodies, and precious jewelry, which they stripped
off for themselves, more than they could carry away; and
they were three days gathering the spoil because there was
so much.

(That's a lot of spoil.)

Listen, God wants us to reap the spoils of our warfare! You win! You get more than bragging rights—you get more than "I survived the mountain; it didn't kill me." You get the spoils! You get the *lan-yap*! And one thing I prayed when I was going through that heartbreak with an ex-boyfriend was, "Lord, don't let me die!" In other words, "Don't let me go down to the pit and never recover!" Somehow, climbing Kilimanjaro was part of my healing process, and making it to the top, as difficult as it was, helped me feel alive! And after a breakup, let's face it...we need something that makes us feel alive! And excited again!

Actually, I think making it to the summit of Kilimanjaro was God letting me know that my warfare was over—my years of heartbreak were over; I was free! I got my heart back! And in the process, I also got stronger! I got some new muscles! I was leaner! Tougher! More courageous than ever before because I didn't turn back. And then, just like God, I end up honeymooning in Africa, and Bill and I get to see Kilimanjaro on our way back to the airport with a driver named "God Listened." You can't make this stuff up.

No matter what you're facing, no matter how steep the climb, refuse to quit! Don't be one of those who turn back. Refuse to give into fear! Finish your race! And reap the spoils! You're closer than you think! You didn't miss it.

26

Back to the Summit

"The mountains are calling and I must go."

—John Muir

Three long years had gone by since I'd hiked to the top of my beloved Old Rag Mountain; the peak is part of the majestic Blue Ridge Mountains and the most popular hike in the Shenandoah National Park. Don't get me wrong; they'd been great years! Amazing years! As you know, Bill proposed to me at the top of Old Rag on September 1, 2018, followed by my dream wedding and honeymoon just five months later—but then, a few months after we got married, I landed in the hospital. A couple of months prior to my unexpected hospital visit, I knew I hadn't been feeling as energetic as I had in the past, but I just figured it was due to all the new and exciting changes that go along with being a newlywed. One day after work, I went out for my usual two-mile fast-paced power walk in my neighborhood, and on the way home, I literally couldn't put one foot in front of the other. I felt like a car that had suddenly run out of gas and was now stranded in the middle of nowhere. It was scary because I was still nearly a mile from home. I leaned forward and put my hands on my knees to rest the way runners do after a hard run. I prayed, "Lord, please, help me to get home." I stood back up and slowly put one foot in front of the other and, by the grace of God, made it home. I chalked it up to too much caffeine or not enough sleep. I'd always been so healthy and strong and couldn't imagine that there was anything truly wrong with me. But this pattern of suddenly running out of energy, having severe low-blood sugar, despite eating, and feeling so exhausted that I could barely get through a newscast or walk across the room continued until one day in late July, it finally came to a head.

Feeling too weak to drive, I begged my friend and colleague Sherry to take me to the hospital. Sherry stayed with me as we waited to see the doctor. When the young, handsome doctor arrived and asked me to explain my systems, I started to cry—not sure how to describe what it feels like to be at the anchor desk and not have enough energy to read the teleprompter or walk across the room. It felt like the "life force"—whatever was keeping me alive—was leaving my body. I was scared. I had just gotten married! I worried, "What will Bill think of me?" I didn't want to be a disappointment to him. They put me through a number of tests, checking every system and organ. Later, they moved me from the ER to a hospital room, the first time I'd spent the night in a hospital since I was born! When Bill arrived, I was so happy to see him and look into his blue eyes, which were so filled with love and kindness. He sat in a chair close to my bed and held my hand. Inwardly though, I felt insecure, wondering if he was thinking, *Man, what did I get myself into?* There was no evidence of that, though. I wanted to be strong for him, but in that moment, I was anything but, and he was the strong one. I needed him. I had to admit it to myself—*I needed him!* I wasn't the independent single girl who didn't need anyone anymore. Our wedding vows, "in sickness and in health," were already being tested. Why was this happening?

A few hours later, Bill left to go home and get some rest, and I was alone except for the nurse, who came in and out frequently to check on me. That night, I put some soothing worship music on my phone and let it minister to my spirit as I tried to sleep. Hopefully tomorrow, there would be good news.

The next morning, around 9 a.m., a pretty lady doctor with long brown hair and a white coat walked in. She introduced herself and told me that my blood tests were in, and they had a diagnosis. "You have low thyroid, also known as Hashimoto's disease," she said.

I was relieved it wasn't something worse. They wanted me to try a drug called levothyroxine, so I did. I felt worse. I tried several variations of that drug, plus a couple of others, and they all made me feel worse, so I decided to try and heal naturally with good food and rest. That summer, it was a big victory if I could just walk around the block or bike for twenty minutes. Although my husband could not have been more supportive, I still felt guilty for "falling apart" right after we got married; I wanted to have my strength back, and I missed my favorite past-time—hiking.

In the months that followed, I slowly regained my strength but had to be very careful about food, caffeine (which stressed my adrenaline glands), and not exercising too strenuously, which was the most frustrating part, as I really missed those good sweaty workouts.

The silver lining was I was falling more in love with my husband. I realized that real love was more than just romance. Although I am the queen of romance—just ask my husband—God was showing me what real love was: in sickness and in health, in good times and in bad, you love each other; you don't run away; you stay, and you support, and you pray and not just because you made a commitment to do these things but because now the two have become one. I was falling in love with my husband in such a much deeper way than I ever could have without this "trial or test." And yes, he would joke with me and say, "I thought I married a mountain climber!" And I would answer, "You did! But then I got married!"

In the following years, we did some shorter hikes like Mary's Rock and Hawksbill Loop in the Shenandoah National Park but kept our distance from my favorite, Old Rag—a longer and more strenuous hike—until Labor Day, 2021.

It wasn't even on the agenda that weekend; we would hike White Oak Canyon, another favorite not far from Old Rag, which is also known for its beautiful waterfalls—a lower falls and an upper falls. In the summer, you can bathe in the pools created by the water flowing down from the falls, although the mountain water is still so cold that it takes your breath away. White Oak is beautiful but not nearly as challenging or exciting as Old Rag and, therefore, not quite as fulfilling, but I just didn't know if I was ready for Old Rag. So after hiking White Oak that Sunday, we drove by Old Rag, and I blew her a kiss and a prayer, but a visit to the summit still seemed a remote possibility.

The next morning, we met Jim, the owner of the rustic lodge we were staying in. After sharing the story of our engagement at the top of Old Rag, he asked us if we knew about the lesser-known route up the mountain—a backway to the summit, so to speak—still challenging but a bit shorter than the usual six hours roundtrip. After probably more than a hundred summits on Old Rag, I had not heard of this route. Curious, my husband and I drove to the remote parking lot Jim mentioned that led to this back way up the mountain. There were only fifteen parking spaces, and someone was leaving just as we arrived! Maybe it was a sign we were really supposed to do this. Still a bit nervous, Bill and I agreed that we would go as far as I could with no pressure to reach the top.

After almost a mile of steep uphill climbing, we saw the trailhead sign for Old Rag—I cried. Could this be a "God setup"? So many emotions washed over me. Only God had seen my journal entries praying that I could hike Old Rag again this year! Still, I was cautious; I didn't want to have a thyroid "melt-down" where I lost all my energy and couldn't make it down the mountain. I remembered what I learned climbing Mount Kilimanjaro years earlier, *pole, pole*—which in Swahili means slowly, slowly. Slow and steady wins the race. I would take my time, enjoy nature, and go as far as I could. Truthfully, I wasn't feeling that great. I would say my energy level was about a six, but we had plenty of water, and I had eaten a big breakfast and then a sandwich before we started, so I felt confident that at least I had consumed enough calories for the climb.

About halfway up the mountain, we stopped at one of the two shelters, which thankfully had an outhouse. While inside, I prayed for strength for the climb and wisdom to know how far to go. Shortly afterward, we ran into a nice couple coming down the mountain who mentioned that, according to their tracking device, we were one point two miles from the summit. Suddenly, my energy level perked up to about a nine! Hope and new strength flooded my body. It reminded me of summit night on Kilimanjaro when I froze with fear, and my guide said, "This is the place most people turn around." Once again, I didn't want to be one of those who turned back in fear.

We forged on—encouraged by those who had already stood on the summit and were making their way down. "You're almost there!" we heard a lot, even when it wasn't quite true, but it still helped.

About an hour later, we stood on the summit of Old Rag, enjoyed the amazing view we had earned, and then sat on the same rock where Bill had proposed to me. The lesson I learned is that while we may look at our limitations, God is able to make a way where there seems to be no way! Take the limits off yourself because you serve a limitless God—the summit awaits. You didn't miss it!

27

It's Your Turn

"You will arise and have compassion on Zion,
"for it is time to show favor to her;
"the appointed time has come."

Psalm 102:13 (NIV)

Does God care about who you will spend the rest of your life with or even about giving you the desires of your heart for a mate? I can tell you—He does! And more than you know. After all, marriage and romance were God's ideas—read Song of Solomon if you need a reminder that God is into romance.

However, God is a God of order and perfect timing. And I know many of you are so tired of hearing that God's timing is perfect and that if you just wait a little longer...but I am living proof that no matter how old or how long you've waited, God will show up, show off, and give you the desires of your heart for a mate if you don't give up.

He's also a God of compassion and will not require you to wait one more minute than is necessary to fulfill His perfect will in your life. I remember so clearly God saying to me, "When you're ready, there he'll be," and I was over fifty years old! But God knows you better than you know yourself, and in His mercy, He won't bless you until you are ready.

"Therefore, the Lord will wait, that He may be gracious to you; And therefore, He will be exalted, that He may have mercy on you For the Lord is a God of justice; Blessed are all those who wait for Him" (Isaiah 30:18).

But the good news is after the wait comes the blessing.

On October 5, 2018—while still lying in bed, I asked the Lord for a word, and I clearly heard, "It's your turn."

Bill and I had only been engaged for six weeks, and God was reminding me it was my turn! Finally! After celebrating the weddings of my two beloved sisters as well as countless friends, it was now my turn for love, romance, a wedding, a honeymoon, and much more. To be honest, I couldn't wait for all the parties and bridal showers—and I had three! My sister, Jean Anne, threw me a fabulous bridal shower in Washington, DC, complete with a chocolate cake with the words "God is faithful" written in red icing and a limo ride to a fabulous DC hotel with some of my closest girlfriends and family—the '80s music was blasting as we sang and laughed and celebrated well past midnight. Then, the ladies at CBN blessed me with a beautiful shower with precious gifts and prayers, and my best friend Rhonda hosted a bridal tea for me at the cutest little tea house in New Orleans! It was truly my turn!

Only Believe

God is no respecter of persons. What He did for Bill and me—He can and will do for you. What is required of you?

Faith. Only believe. *"Delight yourself also in the Lord, And He shall give you the desires of your heart"* (Psalm 37:4).

Some of you have been waiting for so long that your heart is "sick." *"Hope deferred makes the heart sick, but when the desire comes, it is a tree of life"* (Proverbs 13:12).

New Hope

If you're reading this, I believe God wants to break off hope deferred and the weariness caused by waiting. He wants to breathe new hope and faith into your heart so you'll be ready and able to receive all that God has for you. After all, you must have hope before you can have faith. The Bible says, *"Faith is the substance of things hoped for, the evidence of things not seen"* (Hebrews 11:1).

Shortly after I was married, I was invited to speak to a large group of women in California at the Ascend Women's Conference hosted by my good friend Brenda Epperson Moore. The Lord told me on the airplane ride the day before to invite the women to the front of the stage after I was done speaking because He wanted to break off hope deferred from those whose hearts were "sick" from waiting on His promises. I heard God say, "I will give you a word for them, and I will breathe on them." I'm a charismatic Christian, and I love how God works supernaturally to deliver us, empower us, and give us hope, but

I've got to be honest—this was new for me. I had done plenty of speaking but never before invited women to the altar afterward for a supernatural touch from the Father. I was both nervous and excited.

The next day, when I was finished with my main talk, I decided to act like I'd done this a million times, and I asked anyone who wanted to be delivered from hope deferred to come forward. To my surprise, more than half of the women immediately rushed toward the stage. I began to pray over them, "Father God, I ask You to break off hope deferred and the chains of disappointment and despair from those who've been waiting a long time or have been hurt in past relationships. Lord, release Your healing balm to renew their hearts and minds and bring a fresh new wind of joy to Your daughters. Give them joy in the waiting! Let them have fun while they wait!"

Tears began to flow; heaviness lifted; hope and joy were restored—something supernatural was going on, and it had nothing to do with me. The presence of the Lord was tangible, and women were being set free. It was marvelous. I left the stage and began laying hands and ministering to the women one by one. I'm still in awe of what God did that day for those precious women in California. But that's God's heart for you and for me—and what He did for them, He can and will do for you. He wants you free of hope deferred so you can believe again, hope again, and start expecting His best.

A Season of Breakthrough

If you're reading this, I believe your season of breakthrough is here! You've been waiting a long time—you've been patient, or at least, you haven't given up. God is pleased with you. He's pleased with your faith, and He wants to give you more than you're asking for. If that's you, take courage! God is breathing on you! Infusing you with fresh hope! And new strength to reach the summit where the promises are! I believe your faith is releasing your future blessings even now, and you will see the fruit of your prayers in the land of the living.

God Is Removing the Veil

When I was single, I sometimes thought, *There must be a veil over me because I feel invisible, like no one of the opposite sex can see me.* Well, I believe there was a supernatural veil over me, but it was for my protection, not because God was punishing me. But there comes a time when the veil needs to be lifted—and for many of you, that time has come.

I pray for those who have felt invisible during their season of waiting—*Father, it's time to remove the veil!* The veil was meant to protect you from the counterfeits, but now it is no longer needed. Father, thank You for removing the veils so Your daughters and sons can be seen by their intended. I believe in the power of prophetic action prayers, so right now, take a moment to lift the invisible veil from your face. I did this on February 14, 2017, and met my husband four months later! God doesn't use formulas, but He is moved by our faith—in fact, you can't please Him without it, so Lord, we thank You for removing the veils!

Divorced and Widows

For the widows, God has not forgotten you. He has seen your tears. Many of you had wonderful husbands and marriages in the past and feel a little guilty for even asking the Lord to bring someone new, but God says to you, "Prepare! I am the God of the double portion and double honor, and I often save the best for last!" "*So I will restore to you the years that the swarming locust has eaten*" (Joel 2:25). This goes for divorced people too. God can give you a second chance and a new beginning—trust Him! He wants to give you the desires of your heart. He did that for my husband, and He will do it for you too.

Men

For the men, God says, "Rise up!" Rise up as the hunters and the pursuers that you are! "*He who finds a wife finds a good thing and receives favor from the Lord!*" (Proverbs 18:22). Notice it's the men who "find" and who seek out the wife. And for the sake of all the single women out there, please stop fearing rejection. I know that's easier said than done, but it's your job to ask us out, not the other way around. Not every pursuit will be victorious; you don't catch a fish every time you go fishing—and my husband doesn't get a trophy buck or shoot a deer every time he goes hunting—but if you don't give up, you will be victorious and win the prize.

CHAPTER 27: IT'S YOUR TURN

Get Ready!

And to those who've been waiting for years, even decades, patiently waiting (like I did) and not giving up hope, God says, "Get ready!" It's your turn. Due season is here! Ladies, if you were expecting guests, you would probably clean your house and put extra plates on the table or even buy a new dress. Men, you might wash and wax your car or truck or get a haircut. My point is waiting doesn't have to be idle—or passive. You can get ready now!

Ask yourself, *Am I ready if he or she walks through the door? How is my spiritual health? My physical, emotional, and financial health?* And I'm not saying you have to be the perfect size or have a "fat" 401K—I'm asking, would you marry you? If not, make the changes you need to be ready. First, take care of your spiritual health. Read your Bible, pray, journal, stay connected to the Father, listen to His voice, and heed His advice. Secondly, get out of debt; you don't want to bring a lot of debt into a marriage if you can avoid it. Also, take care of your body; it's the temple of the Holy Spirit, and if you're praying to meet someone who's fit and in shape, make sure you're in shape, too, or working toward that goal. We can all eat better and exercise more, including me! And finally, this is so important—pursue your passions while you're waiting! Don't put your life on hold just because you're single. Do what you love and what brings you joy. These are things we should be doing whether we are single or married. And as you prepare for the blessing of that special someone—it will activate your faith, and faith and expectation, as I've mentioned, are what release the promises of God in your life.

"Therefore, I say to you, whatever things you ask when you pray, believe that you receive them, and you will have them" (Mark 11:24).

I know what it's like to wait, and I know what's it like to have your prayers answered after you've waited, and I can tell you, my friends—it's worth the wait. Don't throw in the towel now when you're so close to the promise.

I believe many of you reading this right now will be dating, engaged, or even married much sooner than you think! Why? Because, as I've said many times, God is no respecter of persons, and what He did for Bill and me, He can and will do for you! Keep climbing the mountain of hope, keep believing, and keep declaring God's promises over your life...

It's your turn! You didn't miss it!

The Passing of the Baton

"But those who hope in the Lord will renew their strength. They will soar on wings like eagles; they will run and not grow weary, they will walk and not be faint."

Isaiah 40:31

Dear reader,

When I wrote the last chapter, "It's Your Turn," I got such a strong sense of passing the baton to you and those who are still waiting. I ran track in high school, and I remember during the relay races keeping my arm stretched as far as it would go behind my back so the runner coming up behind me could easily place the baton in my hand. There was an adrenaline rush as I anticipated feeling that baton hit the palm of my hand, my fingers grasping it as if my life depended on it, and then running with all my might until I could place that same baton in the next runner's hand.

Right now, I'm placing the baton in your hand. You've been waiting patiently, expectantly, and faithfully. You're ready to run! It's your turn! And in this baton you now hold is everything you need to wait on God's perfect timing—*faith, hope, expectancy, and joy.*

"But those who hope in the Lord will renew their strength. They will soar on wings like eagles; they will run and not grow weary, they will walk and not be faint" (Isaiah 40:31, NIV).

You Didn't Miss It!

Printed in the USA
CPSIA information can be obtained
at www.ICGtesting.com
CBHW071547150824
13127CB00014B/605

9 798887 387314